The Complete Terrace Book

How to Design, Build, Furnish,

The Complete Terrace Book

Plant and Enjoy Your Terrace, Patio, Lanai, Deck, Porch, Atrium or Engawa

Stanley Schuler

Collier Books
A Division of Macmillan Publishing Co., Inc.
New York

Collier Macmillan Publishers
London

All photographs by the author except as noted.
Some of them appear in an earlier book,
America's Great Private Gardens.

Macmillan Publishing Co., Inc.
866 Third Avenue, New York, N. Y. 10022
Collier-Macmillan Canada Ltd.

Library of Congress Cataloging in Publication Data

Schuler, Stanley.
The complete terrace book.

1. Decks (Architecture, Domestic) 2. Patio gar-
dening. I. Title.
TH4970.S38   643′.55   73-22529
ISBN 0-02-063710-1 (pbk.)

FIRST COLLIER BOOKS EDITION 1974

The Complete Terrace Book is also published in a hardcover edition by
Macmillan Publishing Co., Inc.

Printed in the United States of America

Contents

The Complete Terrace Book

1 Building to a Purpose

There is a widespread impression that the terrace is a California invention of the twentieth century. Nothing could be further from the truth. Countless centuries ago wealthy Chinese, Egyptians and Persians, among others, were building terraces. True, they didn't use the word *terrace*, and the terraces didn't always look like a modern terrace. But they were built and used for the same purpose: to allow the homeowner to live outdoors when he chose.

Today this desire is more urgently felt than ever before. As a result, the terrace has become one of the most important rooms in the house.

I call it a room because, even though it may not have roof or walls, that's what it is: a space for living. If you prefer to call it a patio, lanai, porch, deck, gallery, atrium, ramada, glorieta, or engawa, that's all right with me. There are slight differences in design or construction, but they are all the same thing: a space for living outdoors.

Is there anyone who doesn't want this?

The ancients did. So did the early padres of California. Their missions had glorious courts and cloisters for the enjoyment and contemplation of nature.

My family's home in Mississippi—circa 1840—has two enormous galleries, and I am sure that in pre-Civil War summers they were well populated with old and young seeking some escape from the heat.

My grandfather Schuler's little summer house in Massachusetts had a porch that I remember as clearly as yesterday. It overlooked a country road and just beyond that a little river which we crossed in a rowboat to pick wild berries in the woods and meadows beyond. We didn't do much sitting around on the porch except on Sundays. But we ate there almost every day. Wild fruits and fresh vegetables from the garden, and fish and shellfish from Buzzards Bay and still-warm, creamy milk from Jack Noon's farm up the road.

There were terraces or porches on all of my family's houses outside Philadelphia, but I don't recall them very well. Yet as I think back, I find I recall them better than most of the rooms inside the houses.

Then there was the house my parents rented briefly before

World War II. It had been built by a famous University of California geologist smack on top of the San Andreas Fault. The floors, walls (including interior walls) and roof deck were made of reinforced concrete of great thickness. But the feature of the house was a second-floor deck or porch—I don't know what to call it—that was cantilevered out from the southwest wall so you could bask in the sun and survey a large part of San Francisco Bay. We lived there whenever the Bay Area's weather permitted. And as luck would have it, nobody ever fell off even though the entire front of the terrace was unwalled and unfenced.

The same house had two other second-floor balconies worth mentioning because they might give you some ideas. These did have walls and roofs, and I suppose they were meant to be sleeping porches—if anyone can imagine sleeping outdoors in the Bay Area. But the most intriguing feature of each porch was a large concrete-walled shower stall. Why anybody used these I don't know, but on my visits there I did.

All of the houses my wife Elizabeth and I have owned have had terraces, and they have been given hard use. We couldn't have lived happily without them because they enabled us to sit and feast on the beauties of the outdoor world and they inspired some

Corner of a magnificent terrace built for family relaxation, entertaining and enjoyment of a sweeping view and nearby swimming pool. Other pictures on opposite page, Jonathan Isleib, designer.

A terrace for sunbathing
is walled off from the
large terrace in the
first picture.

And a third terrace—
actually a high-level deck—
for eating is at the far end
of the house. The picture is
taken looking up through the
railing at the deck, which is
partially roofed with a
plastic bubble.

Author's large terrace as seen from the flower garden. The covered gallery at the back is the main passageway between house and garage (unseen at right). Wading pool in the foreground reflects the sky and overhanging pin oaks.

of the best parties we ever gave (and I think it's fair to say that Elizabeth is famed for her parties).

Our present home, which we bought five years ago, has three terraces plus a deck around the swimming pool which is used as a terrace even when no one is swimming. The previous owners created the terraces and we have done almost nothing to change them. I have no idea how they used them; but for us, each of the three has a personality and is used in a rather definite way.

Opening off the south side of our bedroom is an open brick terrace. Even in Connecticut we can use it from mid-March to Thanksgiving because it is warmed by the sun the better part of the day. It's our favorite place to read the Sunday papers while enjoying a noontime cocktail.

A flagstone terrace is set in the L between the living room and dining room. From it we can look to the end of the lawn and to the swimming pool beyond and to the flower garden south of the

4

lawn. Since about a third of the terrace is roofed, we can use it on inclement, but not too inclement, days as a gathering place for drinks with family or a few friends. But mainly the open part of the terrace is our place to eat lunch and dinner and sometimes breakfast during the summer.

Finally, there is a large open terrace set in a U between the end of the dining room, garage and a connecting covered gallery. It overlooks the lawn and flower garden and is itself edged with shrubbery borders on the dining room and garage sides. An old sycamore protects it from the worst of the sun. Here we do most of our outdoor entertaining. And on the occasion of our youngest daughter's wedding, the terrace—which is paved with large slates surrounded by bricks—became a charming dance floor.

My purpose in regaling you with Schuler terraces of present and past is not to impress you but to make a point: Whatever it is called, a terrace should serve a purpose if it is to be successful. Or, putting it another way, when you set out to build or remodel a terrace, the first thing you must decide is what you want it for, how you want to use it.

There are possibilities galore. Here are some of them, along with the requirements that they impose:

A terrace for dining, entertaining and just plain sitting to drink in the beauties of the surrounding garden. In the background, a pair of fountains bring to the scene the music of water splattering into a pool.

Just Relaxing   Under this heading come such things as doing nothing, thinking, reading, talking. A terrace for this purpose usually should be both sunny and shady. It need not be protected against rain; but since a terrace can be unusually delightful on a warm rainy day or evening, I think it should be at least partially roofed. Protection against wind is essential, and so is a pleasant outlook (but note that a pleasant outlook is not necessarily a spectacular view).

Eating   For this you want mostly shade but some occasional sun. Protection from rain and wind is a must. Ditto a pleasant outlook. For convenience, the terrace should be close to the kitchen and, secondarily, to the dining room.

Entertaining   The requirements are similar to those for an eating terrace, but the terrace should be closer to the dining room than to the kitchen because, in borderline weather, some guests will choose to eat indoors.

Dancing   Twenty and thirty years ago, dancing was a popular pastime in the home. Perhaps it still is with you. If so, a terrace for dancing should be shady, protected from rain and wind and well protected from the neighbors. Place it close to the family room or living room, and put down a very smooth pavement.

Swimming   Maximum sunlight is essential, but you also need a shady area to which you can escape. There must also be protection from the wind. The terrace—or at least the pool area—should be close to the kitchen (so the housewife can keep an eye on the children) or bedrooms (where there are bathroom facilities and clothes can be changed). It should definitely not be close to the living area because it ruins use of the area by nonswimmers.

Games   It doesn't make much difference whether the games are to be played by you, your children or both: you need sun and shade, protection from rain and wind. Locate the terrace anywhere close to the living area of the house.

Stargazing   I discovered the excitement of astronomy at our previous house, which we built in the middle of a hilltop meadow. The view from

6

the terrace at night was immense. You need the same kind of location to become a stargazer, too. Set the terrace well out from the house so the roof doesn't interfere with the view. Wind protection is highly desirable, provided that it doesn't cut into the view.

Napping

Here you want shade, seclusion and excellent protection from rain and wind.

Sunbathing

Full sun, privacy and as little wind as possible.

Growing Tropical Plants

Requirements vary somewhat, but as a rule, the terrace must have dappled shade and be well protected against wind.

Welcoming People

One type of entrance terrace is unique in that it is never occupied except by people coming and going from the house. Its primary purpose is to extend a welcome—just as the front hall in the house extends a welcome—and perhaps to give protection from

Simple but inviting entrance terrace welcomes visitors and gives them protection against rain and snow. (PHOTO BY JOHN D. ECCLES)

the weather. Such a terrace can be sunny, shady or both; open to the sky or covered. It is usually surrounded by a wall, fence or dense plantings to give it privacy from the street and to serve as a warning to strangers that they are not really wanted within.

The other type of entrance terrace is an ordinary relaxing terrace which happens to be in the front of the house, usually

7

This is the most exciting yet restful terrace I have ever seen—not because the terrace itself is spectacular but because it is centered in a vast concrete garden with splendid fountains and water running everywhere. Designed by landscape architect Lawrence Halprin, it is a modern version of the fabulous Moorish water gardens.

because there is no other place for it. It has the same physical characteristics as a relaxing terrace behind the house.

This listing of requirements for different kinds of terraces makes the principal problem of terrace building immediately evident: it's extremely difficult to build a single terrace which will serve every purpose. Some compromise is almost inevitable: either you give up the idea of using the terrace for a certain purpose or you jigger the design so that it serves all purposes half well.

This is the best argument for building several terraces like the three shown on pages 2 and 3. All of these are part of the same property. One is a vast general living terrace; another, a sunbathing terrace; and a third, a family eating terrace.

Another argument for the multiple-terrace idea is that it allows you to select a terrace to suit the needs and moods of the moment, and also allows the different members of the family to go their separate ways as they wish. This is the arrangement at my home. All three terraces can be used for about the same purposes; but the differences in design and surroundings dictate which we use at a given moment. (By contrast, there is very little difference in the feeling imparted by the three terraces on pages 2 and 3.)

But let's be practical: the more terraces you build, the more money you are going to spend. Many properties are not large enough or laid out to accommodate more than one terrace. Finally, most families don't really need or want more than one terrace— one attractive, comfortable terrace which the whole family can use together.

So I bow to the majority. This book doesn't ignore special-purpose terraces, but the emphasis is on the multipurpose, general living terrace. Or do you prefer to think of it as a patio, lanai, porch, deck, gallery, atrium, ramada, glorieta or engawa?

2 Basic Planning

The best time to plan a terrace is while you're planning the rest of the house. Then you can place it and shape it almost perfectly. It's just another one of the rooms, and as important as any of them.

Planning a terrace for an existing house is usually more difficult because your hands are pretty well tied by the plan of the house and the way the yard and garden have been developed. For example, my youngest daughter Cary and her husband own a house which started out thirty-five years ago as a little Cape Cod Colonial. It had a small but adequate porch off the dining-room end; but twenty years ago new people bought the house and remodeled it extensively. In the process, the porch was walled up. So now there isn't any porch, terrace or what have you, and Cary and Charlie see no simple way of adding one. The logical location for a terrace is behind the kitchen. "But I won't have people tramping through the kitchen to get to it," Cary says. "We've thought about opening up a door through what was the porch and building a terrace off that end of the house; but there's too much shade, and anyway, since we know we're going to be transferred and since we've already put as much money into the house as we can get out of it, we see no point in spending for something that isn't going to be perfect."

Cary's back-door problem is very common, but it has been given little, if any, thought by people who plan and build houses. Most houses—old as well as new—have only two exterior doors: one in front and one in back or at the side. The latter almost always opens off the kitchen; therefore, since the usual location for a terrace is in back or at the side of a house, the kitchen becomes a passageway to it. This causes two problems: kitchen clutter is exposed to guests, and kitchen operations are disrupted by the heavy traffic.

I am well aware that the first problem is not particularly annoying to casual homemakers. For instance, it bothers Cary, who isn't a casual homemaker; but it doesn't bother her oldest sister, who is. But the second problem is serious for all homemakers, although they may become so hardened to it that they are able to brush it aside. Traffic through the kitchen should not be tolerated; yet in summer, traffic from the terrace into and through the kitchen is likely to be horrendous.

So what to do if your house has only a front door and a back door? Answer: Cut another door through the back side of the house and channel traffic to the terrace through that. Or build the terrace in front of the house and use the front door to reach it.

Setbacks   Building codes almost always include requirements controlling the distance that structures must be set back from the front, side and rear lot lines. As a rule, the structures in question are those built above ground level—for example, the house, a detached garage or toolhouse, fences and walls, roofs, decks, porches and steps attached to the house. A piece of pavement—as for a terrace or driveway—does not count. However, building codes are so varied that I cannot possibly make a blanket statement about them here.

For this reason, when you start planning a terrace, one of the first things you should do is to pay a visit to your town building department to learn what, if any, setback rules will control placement of the terrace. (At the same time, you should find out whether you must get a permit to build the terrace.)

For example, suppose your building code requires a minimum setback of 50 ft. from the street and suppose your house is set back exactly this distance. Can you build a terrace in front of the house if that is the best location for it? The answer is probably yes if the terrace is at ground level.

"But what if we build a 6-ft. fence to screen it from the street?" you ask.

Not permitted. The highest fence or wall allowed in a front yard is 3 ft.

"That's no good for privacy," you protest. "Could I plant a tall hedge around the terrace?"

Yes; planting is not affected by setback rules.

Similar but not necessarily identical rules may affect the location and design of a terrace at the back or side of the house. Generally, side-yard and back-yard setbacks are less than front-yard setbacks; and the rules about the height of fences and other structures are less limiting. But, as I said before, these are questions you must answer before you commit yourself to a terrace of particular design in a particular location on your lot.

Orienting the Terrace   It is clear from the list of terrace uses in the preceding chapter
to the Sun   that the sun is rarely essential to your use of a terrace. Indeed, you don't want it at all on one type of terrace. But on the great majority of terraces it is very desirable because it contributes substantially to

pleasure and comfort. In addition, it affects the climate of the terrace in all seasons of the year and this, in turn, affects when you can use the terrace. So you must give long consideration to the relation of the terrace to the sun before you establish its location.

The following are the pros and cons of the principal exposures. All discussions assume that the terrace is to be built right next to the house or other large building.

THE NORTH TERRACE Twenty years ago, when I was running a promotional home-building program for General Electric, a Phoenix architect I hired surprised me by designing a house with a terrace on the north side. I quickly discovered the reason: in a hot southern climate, a north terrace provides your best escape from the seering sun.

Nine years ago when Elizabeth and I built our previous house in Connecticut, other considerations dictated that the terrace should be on the north side; and again to my surprise, we found the location very good. Despite this experience, however, I don't recommend a north terrace except in the Deep South and Southwest.

It worked out for us because the house was in a meadow and the living-room wing directly south of the terrace was only one story high; consequently the sun, riding high in the summer sky, bathed most of the terrace for most of the day. It missed only a narrow strip right next to the living room. But if the living room wing had been two stories high, the sun would have reached only the outer portion of the terrace; and on a cool summer day the shady area would not have been too comfortable. Moral: If you own a two-story house and you can't avoid building a north terrace, set it as far out from the house as possible so that the sun will strike more of it.

The other problem with a north terrace is that, regardless of the height of the house, the sun doesn't get around to it until rather late in the spring and it disappears early in the fall. Thus terrace use is pretty well limited to the summer months.

THE EAST TERRACE Like a north terrace, an east terrace is more desirable in a warm climate than in a cold one. In the morning, when you don't use it very much, the sun warms it up nicely and burns off the dew, so that from noon on it is a very pleasant place to relax unmolested by the blistering sun. As on any other terrace, you may want a roof to keep off rain, but a sunshade is unnecessary. The sky is a benign, bright-blue canopy overhead.

In colder climates, however, an east terrace may cool off too much in the afternoon.

THE WEST TERRACE   Our favorite terrace faced due west. Despite the fact that it was covered by a low roof, the sun penetrated to the back wall and did its best to put out your eyes. On many a day the terrace also became very hot.

West terraces are like that, and it makes no difference where you live. But it's easy to make them bearable and pleasant by erecting some sort of screen to break the slanting sun rays. And they are often usable on winter afternoons when you wouldn't dream of stepping out on an east or north terrace.

THE SOUTH TERRACE   If there is such a thing as a perfect terrace location, the south side of the house comes closest to winning the honors. Even so, it isn't completely perfect because in all except cold climates, the summer sun in the middle of the day is murderous; and you need something to break its force. But this is a comparatively minor objection.

Since it's exposed to the sun in all seasons, the south terrace is usable many days of the year. Even in the North, the snow melts away quickly, the terrace floor dries and you can enjoy a midday snooze.

In spring, summer and fall, the sun reaches the terrace early in the day and leaves it late. As I said, the heat may be more than you can tolerate at noon; but you are never bothered by the same kind of long, low slanting rays that haunt the west terrace and, to some extent, the east terrace.

THE NORTHEAST, SOUTHEAST, SOUTHWEST OR NORTHWEST TERRACE   If your house faces one of the intercardinal points of the compass, the conditions to expect on the terrace will be a mixture of those just discussed. For example, a southeast terrace will have more sun than an east terrace but not as much as a south terrace. It is a desirable location. On the other hand, a northwest terrace is a poor location, for while it has more sun than a north terrace, it's more glary than a west terrace in June and July, when the sun sets in the northwest.

Orienting the Terrace to the Prevailing Wind

A whisper of a breeze is one thing: on hot days you want all you can get, and even on cool days, it does little to upset you. But winds are to be avoided at all costs. Nothing you do on a terrace is helped by them.

14

A northern Vermont terrace on a high hill is also placed in a corner of the house to escape the wind and to capture the warmth of the southern sun. The terrace is surrounded with lush ferns. A brilliant purple clematis climbs the trellis between the windows at left.

It follows that if you live in an area where you can count on a rather strong prevailing wind, you should locate the terrace where it has some protection. This is usually best provided by placing the terrace on the lee side of the house. Better still, if the house is L-shaped, U-shaped or H-shaped, put the terrace in the alcove so it gets protection on two sides. Or if you're building a new house, put the terrace smack in the center surrounded by four walls. This is called an atrium.

Of course, it is quite feasible to build a screen to ward off the winds. But this usually has some drawbacks because, to be effective, the screen must be quite high and so may interfere with the outlook from the terrace.

This lovely, unpretentious terrace is tucked into a corner of the house for protection against the wind.

Orienting the Terrace to a View

Spectacular views inspire terrace building. I am quite sure that if a housing census were taken, it would be found that almost all houses with views have terraces facing the views while a much smaller percentage of houses without views have any terraces at all. This is quite understandable: if you have a view, you want to enjoy it, and the best way to do this is to walk outdoors where there is nothing to block or restrict what you see.

But unfortunately, the view may be directly to the west or it may be the source of a howling wind. What then?

The wind you can cope with fairly successfully by erecting a wall of glass or plastic. But the setting sun is beyond control. You either accept it or you build the terrace somewhere else. Before

A delightful outlook influences terrace placement as much as a spectacular view. What could be pleasanter than this tropical setting—which happens to be in Detroit?

taking either action, however, you ought to test the situation for a year to determine how much the sun really would upset you if you built the terrace on the west side of the house. In other words, clear space for the terrace and set out furniture; but don't pave the area until you're satisfied that the view is more important than your discomfort.

Of course, if your home does not enjoy a view in any direction, this discussion may seem academic. But you should not consider it in this light because every terrace should have a pleasant outlook even though it doesn't have an honest-to-goodness view. This is one way in which a terrace differs from a living room or family room. If an indoor room has ordinary windows (not big picture windows), a pleasant outlook is not vital because you cannot see very much through the windows and, if you want to, you can draw draperies across what you do see. But except for atriums and terraces that are completely walled for privacy, terraces are open to the world. You can see far beyond their borders, and what you see should be pleasingly attractive.

To me, this is so logical, so important that I cannot for the life of me understand why numerous terraces have such dreary surroundings. The owners must be the same people as those who litter the countryside. They are completely insensitive to beauty.

Enough, however, is enough. The whole business of giving a terrace a pleasant outlook and surroundings is discussed at greater length in chapter 17.

Accommodating the Terrace to the House

The floor plan and shape of your house have an obvious influence not only on the location of your terrace but also on its size and shape. But there are no rules to guide you in relating terrace to house, just a few generalities:

1. Except for a sunbathing and napping terrace, the terrace should be close to the living area of the house. It doesn't make a great deal of difference, however, whether you step out on it from the living room, dining room or family room.

2. A terrace used for eating and entertaining should also be close to the kitchen. But while a door from the kitchen to the terrace is desirable—especially if your family eats many meals on the terrace—it should not be the only door onto the terrace.

3. If a house is not a simple rectangle, placing the terrace in a corner or jog so it will have walls on two or three sides increases

privacy and gives extra protection against winds and possibly the sun.

Accommodating the Terrace to the Lot

Lots which are unusual because of their shape or contours or because of such features as massive rock outcrops or brooks very frequently influence terrace location to a greater extent than any other consideration. They may also influence terrace design and construction.

As a rule, whatever is unusual about the lot forces you to locate the terrace where you don't really want it. For example, a steep hillside may make it so difficult or costly to put a terrace behind the house that you wind up building a deck in front. Similarly, because of an extremely narrow lot, you may have to give up all ideas of placing the terrace in a side yard.

Occasionally, however, the oddity in the lot invites placement of the terrace. For example, the very simple terrace on page 19 was built because the homeowner became captivated by the idea of sitting under the misshapen old apple tree. Similarly, the deck on page 133 was built because the massive granite outcrop under it struck the homeowner as an exciting aerie from which to view the countryside.

There are few nicer places for a terrace than under a shapely shade tree. This is a yellowwood. In some years it drips with fragrant white flower clusters.

A picturesque old apple tree was the reason for this ever-so-simple terrace.

Accommodating the Terrace to Neighboring Properties

The problem here is to gain privacy from the terrace while shielding your neighbors from it. This is most easily done by placing the terrace as far from the lot lines as possible; but perhaps for some reason you can't do this or don't want to. Then the only solution is to plant a hedge or build a wall or fence. But while this will cut off the neighbors' view of the terrace, it doesn't prevent them from driving you crazy with their noise or you from driving them crazy with your noise.

The only way to control sound transmission between neighboring properties is to put as much space as possible between the sources of noise.

Arriving at the Final Answer

Even if you're building a new house, the location of the terrace must as a rule be something of a compromise. To escape the wind, for instance, you may have to give up a little sunlight. Or to have privacy, you can't put the terrace as close to the kitchen as you'd like.

19

This may cause some unhappiness; but in the long run, the slight deficiencies of the terrace won't make an awful lot of difference to you. At least that's true if you have done your planning carefully. Terraces usually turn out badly only when the owners rush into their construction without looking at all the pros and cons and possibilities.

The other reason why the initial shortcomings of a terrace are likely not to seem so dreadful after a while is that plants around the terrace grow; and as they do, the terrace changes whether you like it or not. Our large terrace is an example. Five years ago, the terrace was much sunnier than it is today. The change has come because the sycamore at one corner has grown up and out to such an extent that we are beginning to think about having it taken down.

The Terrace Away from the House

There are good reasons why you might build your terrace at a distance from the house rather than next to it: to get more sun or shade; to capture a view; to find privacy; to take advantage of an entrancing feature of the property. But while you may gain certain advantages, you will lose others which are peculiar to next-to-the-house terraces:

You're much farther from the telephone, front door and bathroom.

You cannot serve meals on the terrace so easily.

You may get caught in the rain.

You may be out of hearing range of infants, invalids and elderly parents in the house.

You may have a treacherous walk to the terrace.

I personally don't consider these to be arguments against building a distant terrace; but I do think they are arguments in favor of building two terraces—one far, the other near.

Be that as it may, almost the same considerations enter into the placement of a distant terrace as in the placement of a house-side terrace: the sun, wind, view, neighbors and unusual aspects of your lot.

3 Terrace Planning Continued

One of the hardest things about planning a terrace is to figure out its size, and I have yet to come up with any useful rules for simplifying the job.

Part of the problem stems from the fact that terrace furniture is usually a bit larger than indoor furniture. Another part of the problem stems from the fact that people seem to throw larger parties outdoors than in, so there's a tendency to size the terrace to the parties rather than to average daily usage.

The handsome, rather formal terrace shown on page 22 is one the owners now consider to be too big. (It measures 18 x 45 ft.) They are not quite certain how it got that way, although they knew they were going to use it for rather sizable parties and they wanted it to be accessible from both kitchen and living room; consequently, they stretched it from one end of the kitchen across the study to a point about midway of the length of the living room. But now they feel that the terrace almost forces them to entertain on an even bigger scale than they expected, because if it isn't very well populated, it feels almost empty. (And, as Elizabeth pointed out to me after we attended a party for some sixty persons, when the terrace is well populated, you don't get around to see everyone you know.)

By contrast, when the terrace on page 23 was completed, the owner thought he had let it get away from him. (It measures 18 x 27 ft.) But now he has concluded that the size is perfect. During normal use, the terrace has enough furniture to make it feel reasonably small and intimate; yet when the larger pieces are removed for a party, it holds thirty persons with ease.

You might say that both of these terraces were accidents—one that turned out well; the other, a little less than well. But I venture to say that there are even more accidents at the low end of the terrace-size scale.

Twice recently we have been to parties which were physically uncomfortable because the terraces were too small. In one case, a huge group persisted in jamming onto a postage-stamp terrace even though it was partially surrounded by an inviting flat lawn on the same level. In the other case, perhaps a dozen persons jammed onto a cantilevered deck which was big enough for only six. (At

To the camera this flagstone terrace doesn't look overly big, but the owners are wondering if it is.

least once during the evening the thought crossed my mind: I wonder if the thing will hold the weight.)

What both homeowners failed to consider is the tendency of people to huddle together not only at large parties but also at small. This you must not fail to do. True, you can point to numerous parties where the guests didn't huddle. But these are a minority; and as a result, terrace builders are on the horns of a dilemma: if you build a terrace that's too small, it's likely to be overcrowded. But if you build a terrace that's too large, people are likely to clump up and make it feel empty.

There can, of course, be a middle ground. One example has been cited. Our large terrace, on pages 24 and 25, is another. Because of the way it's paved, the terrace proper—the part we furnish, though rather sparsely—is only 15 x 17 ft. Three to 12 persons can sit on it and talk across it and feel completely comfortable; there is no straining to see, hear or speak. Yet the terrace instantly expands to 20 x 23 ft. to accommodate a throng, because the narrow walks at the ends and the wide walk at the front, next to the lawn, are extensions of the terrace. (The even wider walk in the gallery at the back of the terrace is never occupied, however, because the pillars and vines somehow impart the feeling of a wall.)

Expansion terraces like this are ideal. But they are a little harder

The owner of this terrace started out thinking it was too large but has since decided it's just right. The terrace is in sight of a country road but is set far enough back so that the owner felt no need to screen it. The lattice structure houses an old well.

to design than those that don't expand. Here are some of the possible approaches:

Start with a rather big terrace but reduce its apparent size for normal living with extra furniture or large furniture.

Use two different paving materials—one to mark the terrace borders for a small gathering; the other to let the terrace grow for large gatherings.

Let the terrace flow into the lawn. Admittedly, this didn't produce the desired results for the owners of the postage-stamp terrace, at least on the occasion of the party we attended. But it has worked out well for us and for others.

Roof part of the terrace. This tends to force small groups to congregate under the roof when they want shade, or out from under the roof when they want sun. Large groups occupy both areas simultaneously.

Give the terrace arms or jogs. For example, the terrace on page 25 has a general resemblance to a yellow crookneck squash. Small groups occupy the neck, where they can look out across a beautiful river. Large groups flow back into the bulbous end of the squash.

Use a fountain, pool, planting bed, etc., in the middle of a large terrace to separate it into two or more small, concentrated but connected areas.

23

My large terrace has a central square of slate surrounded by bricks. This is the part we furnish. But the area can be expanded to accommodate a crowd because it is surrounded by brick walks. A roof deck overlooks the terrace.

On the other hand, three sure ways to prevent expansion of a terrace are to build it on different levels (even though they are only slightly different); to break it into parts by walls or other permanent barriers (even though they are low); and to separate it from the lawn by a wall.

But none of this, I realize, answers the basic question, How big should a terrace be? Whether you design it to expand or not to expand, how much space should you allow?

In another book entitled *All Your Home Building and Remodeling Questions Answered*, I say that the minimum size for a living room is 180 sq. ft. The figure, admittedly, is rather arbitrary; but I didn't dream it up on my own. Others in the building field have used figures very close to this.

In any event, if 180 sq. ft. is adequate for a living room, it is also adequate—*but a minimum*—for a terrace. Note, however, that the length and width of the terrace are just about as important as its area. Long, narrow terraces are much less usable than those which are more nearly square because people seated at the opposite ends find it difficult to converse and because, when the terrace is furnished, there may not be space for people to pass without jostling elbows.

Shaping the Terrace

You can bet on it that if your terrace is square or rectangular, it will not be a failure because of its shape. For one thing, anyone can draw a square or rectangle, so it's impossible to make a mistake in the design. For another thing, the lines of almost all houses are straight, so the terrace blends with them perfectly.

24

This terrace wraps around the house. The furnished area in the background is the part most often occupied; that in the foreground might be called a spill-over area. The area below the living room was fitted into a great outcropping of rock and has a sweeping view of a river many feet below. Thomas G. Coles, architect.

Next to the square or rectangle, the easiest and safest design is a square or rectangle which is rounded at the front or at a corner. The rounded edge gives the terrace a softer look and tends to tie it into the landscape a little better; but, somewhat surprisingly, it also seems to increase the formality of the terrace.

The most difficult terrace design is the free-form, and no one should try it unless he has real skill and training in the design field. In addition, there should be some reason for such a design—perhaps because the contours of the land require it or because there's a rock outcrop that the terrace swirls around; otherwise it is out of place, a stunt.

It's a mistake, however, to make an arbitrary decision for or against a specific terrace design until you try out several. The best way to do this is to start with an accurate plan of your house and the immediately adjacent land. If you have an architect's or builder's plan, use it and add trees, rocks, etc. The only alternative is to make careful measurements of the house and draw a plan of your own on graph paper with four squares to the inch. If you have already established the location of the terrace, let two squares equal 1 ft. Thus, if you build a terrace 24 ft. long, it will take up 12 in. on the graph paper. But if you have not established the terrace location, let one square equal 1 ft. so you can show the entire house plan on the graph paper. (If you're working with an architect's or builder's plan, you must use the scale to which the plan is drawn.)

To draw an accurate plan, it's advisable to get a helper and use a 50-ft. tape. First measure each complete wall section and draw it on the graph paper. Then measure and draw in the position of window and door openings in the vicinity of the terrace because they have some influence on the terrace location and design. Then find the position of trees, permanent shrubs, rocks, etc., and indicate them on the plan. In the case of trees, show the locations of the trunks and also dot in an outline of the canopies, because this helps you to visualize how much of the terrace they will shade.

Once the plan is completed, place a sheet of tracing paper over it and sketch in the terrace. Study this critically. You're concerned not only with the shape and size of the terrace but also with its location. How will the sun strike it? Is it convenient to the rooms in the house? How will it look from inside the house? How will it look from the far side of the yard? Does it have enough privacy? And so on.

Then draw a new sketch on another piece of tracing paper and study this. Continue in this way until you're satisfied that you have created a terrace as nearly perfect as one can expect. Then make an accurate drawing.

If you have built houses or done a fair amount of landscaping, you may well have enough experience in translating plans into realities to go directly from your finished plan to the construction of the terrace. But I advise against this. You will feel a lot more confident in your decision if you lay the terrace out full size in the area where it's to be built.

If the terrace is a straight-line design, stretch white clotheslines between stakes to outline it. (White cord is just as good but doesn't stand out as well.) To show curved and irregular lines, use a truly flexible, light-colored garden hose and string it out on the ground.

Don't trust your eye to lay out 90° corners. Construct a triangle out of narrow boards. The two legs should be exactly 3 and 4 ft. long; the hypotenuse, 5 ft. Lay this on the ground at the sides of the terrace. Place the 3-ft. leg against the house wall. Then stretch clotheslines over the 4-ft. leg to the outer corners of the terrace.

If the outer edge of the terrace is to be rounded, find the midpoint between the sides of the terrace. Then with your board triangle and a long string, establish a line perpendicular to the house over the midpoint. Measure from the house to the farthest point of the rounded edge, and drive a stake (which I'll call A) next to the string. Then tie two slim stakes or steel spikes to the ends of another piece of string equal to half the width of the terrace. Stick one stake (B) a little way into the ground next to stake A; pull the string back tight along the midpoint string; and stick the second stake (C) firmly into the ground. Then swing stake B in an arc from one side of the terrace to the other, and use it to scratch a line in the ground to mark the terrace edge.

A corner is rounded in much the same way. First you must establish the apex of the corner, as if it were not rounded. Place your wooden triangle in the corner; and from the end of the 4-ft. leg, measure along the hypotenuse 2 ft. 10½ in. Make a mark at this point. Then stretch a long string from the apex of the corner over the mark. The string bisects the corner and marks the center of any arc you swing to round the corner. If you want the arc to blend in smoothly with the straight sides of the terrace (it looks best this way), stretch the string serving as a compass from the center line to either of the terrace side lines, and swing the end of the string back and forth until it touches the side line at just one point. Then swing an arc to the other side line, scratching a line in the ground.

As the next to the last step in developing the shape and size of your terrace, cover the ground within the clotheslines and/or hoses with newspapers. "Pave" the area solidly, and shape the papers to the perimeter of the terrace. Now you can see the terrace approximately as it will appear when it is really paved. Once again, study it well from every angle—the rooms overlooking it, the door leading out to it, the lot lines, etc. Finally, walk out on it (try not to muss the papers) and imagine yourself using it.

Does it look as attractive, feel as comfortable and as livable as you want it to be?

Good. Now you're almost ready to start building it.

One Thing More: The Floor Level

You can place your terrace on the same level as the room opening onto it, below the room or a few inches above.

The last elevation is so unusual that we might as well dispose of it quickly. The two most likely reasons for it are that a house is built into a hillside or that the room opening onto the terrace has a sunken floor. In either case, the appearance or usefulness of the terrace need not suffer. The principal problem is to keep water out of the house; but this is not impossible to do.

Terraces on the same level as the house are growing rapidly in popularity. This is partly because you can walk from one area to the other so effortlessly; but this advantage is really of importance only to the elderly and handicapped. The main appeal of the floor-level terrace is that it becomes an extension of the room inside *provided* that the two are separated by floor-to-ceiling windows or sliding glass doors. The transparent wall brings the outdoors in and the indoors out, thus adding to the spaciousness of both areas. In addition, the terrace gains appeal because it is so clearly accessible.

In other words, if you have a terrace at floor level, you should build the house wall of glass. You lose some of the value of the terrace otherwise.

If the terrace is below the room leading to it, however, a wall of glass does not work in the same way. In this case, the terrace never feels like part of the room, so the wall loses value. This is not to say that you might not delight in looking down at the terrace through such a wall. A view down onto a terrace is often more charming than a view straight out at it; but this is usually true only if you are looking down from a considerable elevation.

Because this house is built on a steep hillside, the terrace is 5 ft. below the living room. The raised planting bed to the left of the stone steps hides the foundations of the house and helps to tie the terrace to the house.

Glass walls aside, the obvious disadvantage of a terrace lower than the floor is that you must negotiate steps to go to and from it. True, one or two or even three steps mean nothing to the average healthy person, so there's no need to elevate a terrace just to eliminate them. But if you must build a longer flight of steps, a change in terrace elevation may be indicated.

But here you must come to grips with the practicalities of building.

There are two ways to raise a terrace above the existing grade level. One is to increase the grade level by adding fill, which will serve as the base for the paving. The other is to build a deck.

29

Deck construction is covered in chapter 11. Considered simply from the standpoint of attaching the deck to the house, there are few problems. Whether the walls of the house are made of wood or masonry, the deck can be placed at any level; but it is usually at the level of the room opening onto it.

If you build a conventional terrace on fill, however, you must not allow the terrace paving to extend above the exposed part of the foundation walls unless the house walls are solid masonry (not masonry veneer). Reason: If the paving is higher than the bottom edge of the lowest wood framing member or siding, termites and moisture are likely to attack and destroy the wood in short order. Because of this danger, conventional terraces added to existing frame houses are almost always below floor level. It's only in new construction that a paved terrace can easily be built at floor level.

4 Paving the Terrace

The floor is the most important structural part of every terrace. In fact, it is the only structural part of many terraces. The material you build it with and the way you build it must therefore be studied at length.

Before selecting a paving material, you should come up with satisfactory answers to the following questions about it:

Will it look right with the house and surrounding yard?

Will it be durable?

Will it be easy to clean and maintain?

Will it be safe underfoot?

Will it provide the type of surface that terrace usage will require? (Example: Can children play on it without scratching their knees to ribbons?)

Will it be glary or hot?

Will it permit moisture and oxygen to reach tree, shrub or vine roots growing underneath? (This is important because if you closely surround a plant with solid paving, moisture and oxygen cannot reach the roots, and the plant will die.)

Is the cost within your budget? If not, can you install the paving yourself?

Can the paving material itself and whatever base it is laid on be delivered right to the terrace site? (It's a little too much to expect that you can get by without using a wheelbarrow. But if you're going to put in a concrete base or concrete paving, and if you intend to buy ready-mixed concrete, it's well to consider whether the truck can get to the terrace site.)

General Requirements   Regardless of the paving material used, there are several things you must do or may have to do before and during construction of a terrace floor:

1. If you raise the level of the terrace with fill, you have to decide whether to build retaining walls around the outer edges of the terrace or whether to grade away from the terrace. Generally, walls are used if the terrace is to be raised substantially; but they are also used when a terrace is raised but a few inches. In either case, the walls are built before the space behind them is completely filled in and before the terrace is paved. For how to build walls, see chapter 5.

Grading away from a terrace is usually done when the terrace is raised no more than a couple of feet and the slope is very slight. But sometimes terraces are built at the top of tall, steep banks; and the banks are developed as rock or wall gardens or are supported by railroad ties interplanted with small shrubs or vines.

Whatever approach you take, the fill used must be free of wood and other vegetation which will attract termites and which will eventually rot, allowing the fill to subside. Good fill consists of rock, gravel, concrete rubble and soil. If the upper layers are porous, a concrete slab can be laid directly on top; or if you are laying paving blocks on sand, you need add only an inch of sand. If the fill is not porous, however, it should be topped off with a 4-in. layer of crushed rock to support a concrete slab; or with a 3-in. layer of rock plus 1 in. of sand to support loose-laid paving blocks.

Another step you must take when using fill is to let it settle for about two months after it has been brought up to grade. The settling process can be hastened, however, if you soak the fill with water as you pour it in.

2. If you build a terrace at ground level, the soil must be dug out to a depth equal to the thickness of the paving material plus the base on which it is laid. The figures are given in the sections following. All allow for the terrace floor to be approximately ¼ in. above the ground (not the grass tips) in an adjacent lawn area. If the terrace adjoins a planting bed, however, the paving should be at least 1 in. above the soil in the bed to keep the latter from drifting onto the terrace. In all cases, firm the bottom of the excavation by heavy tamping and, if necessary, by soaking with water. Never pour a concrete slab or lay a sand-and-gravel base on un-firmed soil.

3. All terrace floors must be sloped at least 1 in. in 8 ft. to hasten runoff of water. (On very large terraces, the slope should be 1 in. in 4 ft.) If the terrace is next to the house, the slope must, of course, be away from the house; but if the terrace is distant from the house, the slope can be in any direction. In both cases, however, you must avoid directing the water to an area which can be damaged by it. Above all, do not let the water flow into neighboring properties.

Should it be impossible to slope your terrace so that no damage will be done by the runoff, slope the four sides toward the center and install a drain. This should have a removable grilled top and

*To provide
good drainage, large
rectangular weepholes (to
right of tree in foreground)
have been provided
in this handsome stone
retaining wall, which
rises about 2 ft. above the
level of the terrace floor.*

should be made of 4-in. composition drainpipes leading to a storm sewer, dry well or stream, pond or other natural disposal area.

If terrace walls extend above the paving, install a central floor drain or provide weepholes in the walls. These should be about 4 in. wide to prevent rapid clogging by leaves, twigs and dirt. Space them about 6 to 10 ft. apart if the paving is solid; but wider spacing is adequate if the paving is laid on a sand base which absorbs the water trickling down through.

4. As noted in the previous chapter, if the paving abuts a wall of the house, it must not be higher than any wood used in the wall. Keep it at least 2 in. below the wood.

5. If steps are required from the house down to the terrace, they can be built of wood or masonry. Wood is easier to work with but the resulting product looks and is less permanent. Construction starts after the terrace is paved. Use notched stringers available from a lumber yard, and cut them to rest on the paving and bear against the side of the house, to which they are spiked. Make the treads and risers of 2 x 6s. Unless redwood or cypress is used, all parts of the steps should be saturated with wood preservative before they are assembled.

Masonry steps are constructed before the paving is completed. Build them up from a concrete footing poured on well-compacted soil at least 18 in. below the level of the paving. The footing should be slightly wider and deeper than the steps and about 1 ft. thick. Hire a mason to do the work, because it's rather tricky. The treads should be of the same material as the terrace floor.

Treads for exterior steps must never be less than 11 in. deep; risers, never less than 7 in. high. Fifteen-inch treads and 6-in. risers are far more desirable—not only more attractive but also safer and easier to climb.

Paving with and Without Mortar

A number of paving materials can be laid either in mortar or on a bed of sand and gravel. The latter installation is generally the more attractive because the joints between the pavers are narrower and do not stand out as sharply as gray or white concrete. Furthermore, the slight irregularity of the paving adds to its beauty because the rigidity which characterizes paving laid in concrete is missing.

Other nonesthetic advantages of dry-laid paving include the following: If a paver is damaged, it can be easily lifted out and replaced. You can create planting pockets anywhere. Water and oxygen penetrate to plant roots. And installation is much easier and less expensive.

Whether a dry-laid paving has the durability of that laid in mortar is debatable. I have read that it doesn't in cold climates, but I have seen no evidence to support this. If a sand-and-gravel base is properly prepared, pavers laid on it are not much affected by frost action and usually settle back into place if they are heaved.

On the other hand, weeds and grass can be a nuisance in a dry-laid terrace floor; and if you try to subdue them by placing heavy polyethylene film or 15-lb. building felt under the pavers, you end up by starving tree roots underneath. What's more, you still cannot prevent weeds from sprouting in the sand that fills the joints.

Another drawback of a dry-laid floor is that you must take it up if you decide to close in the terrace to make a room. By contrast, there's nothing to keep you from using a floor laid in mortar as a room floor. (But note that if at the time you build the terrace you are reasonably certain you will ultimately close it in, it's a good idea to place a polyethylene vapor barrier between the ground and the concrete base for the floor.)

Estimating Materials Needed for a Sand-and-gravel Base

The sand may be of any kind. It should be free of soil but the particles need not be uniform in size. For gravel use bank-run gravel, pebbles or crushed rock. The pebbles and rock should be of small size; otherwise much of the sand poured over them will disappear into the interstices.

Buy both materials by the cubic yard or half cubic yard. A cubic yard equals approximately 47,000 cubic inches. To determine how much sand or gravel you need, multiply the square-foot area of the terrace by 144. This gives you the area in square inches. Then multiply by the depth of the base in inches. Round off to the closest thousand and cancel the last three digits. Divide the answer by 47. This tells you how many tenths of a cubic yard you need. Order to the next highest half yard or whole yard.

For example, if your terrace is 200 sq. ft., it measures 28,800 square inches. This rounds off to 29,000, or 29. If you need a 1-in. sand cushion, divide 29 by 47. The answer is 0.6, so you must buy 1 cu. yd. of sand.

If you place a 3-in. base of gravel under the sand, just measure three times the exact amount of sand required. Or if you figure your gravel needs before figuring the sand, multiply 28,800 by 3. That equals 86,400. So divide 86 by 47.

Paving with Artificial Turf

AstroTurf's "Action Surface" is the only type presently available that is recommended for terraces. Made of nylon, the grass is very dense, fine and only ⅜ in. tall. It is the same material that is used on football fields and looks exactly like bent grass or fine-textured Bermuda grass of a deep emerald green. Though expensive, it gives few problems and requires no costly maintenance. It is resistant to fading, mildew, decay, extreme cold, snow and ice. Occasional vacuuming gets out embedded dirt; washing with a hose keeps the color bright. Most stains are removed with detergent solution and a scrubbing brush. Damaged spots can be cut out and patched. However, the turf has a watertight backing and should not be laid too close around trees. It is damaged by fire and careless snow shoveling.

You can lay the turf on bare, well-compacted soil, in which case simply roll it out and don't bother to fasten it down. But it is more commonly laid on a concrete or asphalt base to which it may or may not be fastened with double-faced adhesive tape. For how to build a concrete slab, see "Paving with Flagstones." To prepare an asphalt base, excavate to 4-in. depth and pour in 2 in. of sand which is then covered with 2 in. of blacktop. Level with a rake and compact with a heavy roller which is dampened with water to prevent sticking.

If an extraresilient surface is desired, a shock-absorbing pad can be sandwiched between the turf and base.

Paving with Brick

Although you won't find all of them in every masonry-supply outlet, bricks are available in a wide range of colors and textures and several sizes of rectangles, squares, hexagons and octagons. With the exception of some raw colors and rough textures, all make a beautiful terrace floor. But I think most homeowners will agree that the standard 4 x 8-in. rectangles in soft pinks and rosy reds are the standouts; and since they can be laid in many interesting patterns, the beauty of the finished floor is further enhanced.

New bricks are strong and durable (secondhand bricks are considerably less so); reasonably low in cost; and skidproof unless used in a damp, heavily shaded location, where they develop a coating of moss and become treacherously slippery (this can be corrected—but not permanently—by scrubbing with chlorine bleach). However, they soak up many stains unless treated with a colorless penetrating masonry sealer.

You can lay bricks in concrete, but the ½-in.-wide joints detract from the result; consequently, most terrace floors are now laid dry. It is important to note, however, that the actual size of most bricks is less than 4 x 8 in. (Two of the most common sizes are 3⅝ x 7⅝ and 3¾ x 8.) This means that in order to use some paving patterns, such as basket weave, in which two bricks are perpendicular to a third brick, you must either lay standard bricks in mortar or find a yard which sells bricks with actual dimensions of 4 x 8 in.

Several popular paving patterns are illustrated. Some can be made with bricks of any size. To make the others, you must either lay standard bricks in mortar or buy 4 x 8-in. (actual dimensions) bricks.

Three popular brick-paving patterns. Left to right: common or running bond, basket-weave, and herringbone.

To estimate the number of bricks needed, find the square footage of the area to be covered by bricks laid flat (see next paragraph). If using bricks with an actual dimension of 4 x 8 in., order four and a half bricks to the square foot. If using smaller bricks, order five bricks to the square foot. Buy some extras to allow for breakage.

Bricks around terrace edges next to grass and planting beds (but not next to buildings and walls) should not be laid flat, because they tend to shift and twist. They should, instead, be laid as a soldier course—standing on end and with the wide sides perpendicular to the terrace. To figure the number required, measure the length of each edge in feet and divide by 2.25. (Standard bricks are 2¼ in. thick.)

Lay bricks on a base of 3 in. of gravel topped with 1 in. of sand. If constructing the terrace at ground level, this means you should

Brick paving laid in a running bond on sand. The "patch" in the foreground was deliberately planned to relieve the monotony of bricks running all in one direction on an enormous terrace. The edging in front of the railing is made of Heller's holly.

dig out the earth to a depth of 6 in. Make the excavation slightly larger than the terrace, and then lay out the terrace with twine stretched tightly between stakes and sloped to show the pitch of the paving. Measure carefully so you don't have to cut any more bricks than necessary.

Set the edging bricks first. Pack soil and fill firmly around those in the soldier courses. Edging bricks next to the house and other walls are laid flat, like those in the middle of the terrace.

When the edges are completed, rake the sand fairly smooth at the end of the terrace where you will start laying the bricks. It should come to about an inch below the tops of the edges. Then sprinkle the sand with water and tamp it firm.

Cut a 2 x 4 timber to span the narrow dimension of the terrace and notch the ends to fit over the edging bricks. The notches should be 2 in. deep. This forms a sand leveler. Set it over the edging bricks and draw it forward 12 to 15 in. to level the sand and remove any excess. If low spots remain, add more sand; tamp it; and then level once more.

Lay the bricks on the leveled sand from one terrace edge to the other. If the pattern is a running bond (the commonest pattern), you can start the first row with a whole brick and end with a whole brick. The second row then starts with a half brick and ends with a half brick. An alternative is to start the first row with a whole

38

On this multilevel terrace, bricks are laid in a herringbone pattern in concrete.

brick and end with a half brick; then start the second row with a half brick and end with a whole brick.

The drawings illustrate how other patterns are formed. Note that in a herringbone pattern, the "bones" parallel the sides and the "backbones," in effect, are at a 45° angle to the sides.

To cut bricks, score them on opposite sides with a cold chisel or wide mason's chisel. Then hold the chisel on one line and strike it with a hammer. If the broken edges are rough, rub them together.

In placing each brick, set it down squarely so that the edges or

To lay a brick terrace, put in the edges first, then level the sand base between them with a 2 × 4 sand-leveler.

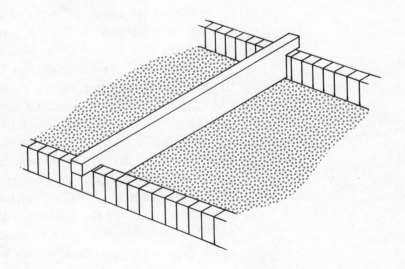

corners do not dent the sand. If it's lower than the adjacent bricks, sprinkle more sand underneath. Tightly butt the ends and sides of adjacent bricks. The joints should be so narrow that you can barely slip a knife blade into them.

After each row of bricks is laid, lay your sand leveler flat side down on top of it, and hammer it down until the ends touch the edging bricks.

After about three rows of bricks are laid, check them with a carpenter's square or a large wooden triangle of the type used to lay out your terrace to make sure they are perpendicular to the edges. Then rake, sprinkle, tamp and level another strip of sand, and lay three more rows of bricks.

As soon as part of the terrace is completed, you can walk on it; but keep back from the unfinished edges.

When all the bricks are laid, sweep sand over them and work it into the joints. Then hose the surface to settle the sand further. When dry, remove the excess but keep it until you're sure you don't need to add more to keep the bricks from wobbling.

Paving with Exposed-aggregate Concrete

Exposed-aggregate concrete is a conventional poured-concrete pavement with small pebbles or stone chips partially embedded in the surface. Unlike concrete used in sidewalks and driveways, it is extremely handsome material which doesn't show stains because of the color and nubby texture of the aggregate. Its carpetlike effect makes it particularly suitable for large terraces; but you should not hesitate to use it on a small terrace, too.

No other paving is stronger or more durable. But it is totally lacking in resiliency and is no fun to walk on barefoot. It also stops water and oxygen from penetrating the ground underneath.

An exposed-aggregate concrete slab should be 4 in. thick. If the soil is porous, compact it well and pour the slab directly on it. But if the soil is dense or if you live in a very cold climate, put a 4-in. layer of crushed rock under the slab.

To simplify construction and eliminate the need for open expansion joints, divide the terrace into 4- or 5-ft. squares with a grid of all-heartwood redwood or cypress 2 x 4s. The outer members of the grid should surround the terrace completely—even where it abuts a wall. Set the timbers with the 2-in. edges upward and nail them together with galvanized-steel spikes. Stick masking tape to the tops to prevent discoloration when the concrete is poured.

Because water runs off the rough surface slowly, slope the entire terrace ¼ in. per foot.

To determine how many cubic feet of concrete are needed, multiply the length of the terrace by the width by 0.33.

The easiest but not the cheapest way to acquire concrete is to buy a ready-mix delivered by truck. But because most companies make large-batch deliveries only, you must be prepared to lay the entire terrace in one day. To do this, you will need several capable helpers.

Renting a cement mixer to mix batches for a few squares at a time may be a better approach. Or, if you want to do things the

Enormous terrace sweeping around a Utah house is paved in exposed-aggregate concrete poured in redwood-framed squares. A large mugo pine takes the place of one square. The clump of native scrub oaks was retained when the terrace was built by partially surrounding them on the house side with a stone wall. Thomas D. Church, landscape architect. (**PHOTOS BY JOHN D. ECCLES**)

hard way, build a low-sided wooden mixing platform measuring about 6 x 8 ft., and mix the concrete with a shovel and hoe.

If you mix your own concrete either with a mixer or by hand, you will need the following:

Type I Portland cement. This is the ordinary cement used for most construction purposes. It comes in 94-lb. bags comprising 1 cu. ft.

Builder's sand. Not sea sand. It must be free of dirt and other debris.

Coarse aggregate—clean pebbles or crushed stones up to 1-in. diameter.

Water.

You will also need to buy whatever type of pebbles, granite screenings, marble chips, etc., you elect to surface the pavement; but these are not mixed with the concrete itself. Ideally they should be quite uniform in size—between ½ and ¾-in. diameter.

The proper proportions for concrete used in paving are 1 sack of cement, 2¼ cu. ft. of sand and 3 cu. ft. of coarse aggregate. After these are thoroughly blended, they should be mixed with a precise amount of water. To determine the amount needed, press some sand together in your hand. If it is bone-dry and falls apart when you open your hand, use 6 gal. of water per sack of cement. If the sand falls apart when you open your hand, use 5½ gal. If the sand holds its shape, use 5 gal. If the sand sparkles and wets your hand, use 4¼ gal.

The table shows how much material you should order to pave several sizes of terraces. To measure the sand and aggregate, build a plywood box with inside measurements of 12 x 12 x 12 in.

After the concrete is mixed, sprinkle the excavation with water until it is well dampened but not puddled. Then pour the concrete into one of the squares. Try not to overload the square so that you are forced to scrape off a lot of excess mortar. Spade the concrete well, especially next to the timbers, to eliminate air pockets.

Strike off the concrete flush with the timbers by laying a 2 x 4 across the square and drawing it from one end to the other. As you do this, saw the 2 x 4 back and forth.

When the concrete in a square is level, scatter the decorative aggregate over it. Cover the entire surface evenly. Then with the flat side of a 2 x 4 pat the aggregate into the concrete until it is completely embedded. When the concrete begins to harden, brush the mortar away from the upper part of the aggregate with a semi-stiff floor brush. As you do so, hose it lightly with water to loosen the concrete.

Cement, Sand and Aggregate Required for Terrace Building

Terrace size (sq. ft.)	Cu. ft. of paving	Cement (sacks)	Sand (cu. ft.)	Coarse aggregate (cu. ft.)
81	27	6¼	14	19
100	33	8	18	24
150	50	12	26	35
200	66	16	35	47
250	83	20	44	59
300	99	24	52	70
400	132	31	69	93
500	165	39	86	116
600	198	50	103	139

Let the concrete cure under damp burlap for a week. Then clean the surface with a solution of 1 part muriatic acid in 9 parts water to remove concrete clinging to the tops of the pebbles.

Paving with Concrete Patio Blocks

Patio blocks are factory-made slabs of concrete 1½ in. thick. They are produced in squares, rectangles, hexagons and special shapes in various sizes, colors and textures. When hexagons and special shapes are used, half-size blocks with one straight edge are needed to square off the edges of a terrace.

Patio blocks are attractive, relatively inexpensive and easy to install. Water goes through the joints into the ground. But they are less strong than other slab- or tile-like pavers, and they stain as readily as poured concrete (which is a good reason for using blocks with a strong texture).

If you use rectangular or square blocks of one size, you can easily estimate the number needed by finding the area of the terrace in square inches and dividing by the square-inch area of a single block. If you use a mixture of sizes or other shapes, however, make an accurate sketch on graph paper showing the position of each block. You will also need the sketch when you build the terrace.

Lay the blocks on a 4-in. base of sand and gravel. The base should be extended several inches beyond the terrace edges to prevent the blocks at the edges from settling or tipping when stepped on. Sprinkle the sand with water and tamp it firm. Then level it with a 2 x 4.

When placing blocks on the sand cushion, take pains to set them flat and check each newly completed row with a spirit level and long 2 x 4 to make sure the blocks are level. Add sand under those that are low. Tamp down those that are high.

Small sizes of concrete patio blocks pave this postage-stamp terrace. They are laid in sand.

Provide ⅛-in. joints between blocks, and when the terrace is completed, sweep fine sand into them and settle it with water. If you elect to coat the blocks with a penetrating masonry sealer to prevent staining, this should be applied and allowed to dry before the joints are filled.

Where the terrace adjoins a planting bed, sink a 3- or 4-in.-high edging of rigid metal or redwood into the ground against the edges of the blocks. This will keep them from drifting into the bed.

44

Paving with Cut Stone Blocks

These are ever so handsome, small, slightly irregular cubes of granite, sandstone, etc. The color depends on the type of stone. The texture is variable, usually rough, but delightful.

A terrace floor made with cut stone blocks is very strong and durable (although limestone may weather rapidly in city atmospheres). Resistance to stains is generally good. Water seeps through the joints to plant roots. But because of the roughness of the surface and the unevenness of the joints, sweeping is difficult.

Because of the variation in block sizes and because blocks of any given style are not uniform in size, the only way to figure how many you need is to determine the square-inch area of the terrace, decide which style of block you will use, and let the supplier estimate your requirements.

Construct the terrace like a brick terrace on a sand-and-gravel base.

If the blocks you use are rectangles, set those at the open edges of the terrace vertically. But if the blocks are cubes, pick out those that are deepest and set them about ½ in. deep in a ribbon of concrete. This should be about 4 in. deep and 4 in. wide. Allow it to set 24 hours before laying blocks within the edges.

Variation in the depth of blocks slows their placement and makes it difficult to achieve a level surface. About the only thing you can do after dampening and tamping the sand base is to strike it off with a sand leveler about ¼ in. higher than the thickness of the thinnest block. (For example, if the thinnest block is 2¾ in. thick, the sand base should be leveled 2½ in. below the tops of the edging blocks.) Then, as you set thicker blocks, you must either pound them into the sand or scoop out a little sand for them.

In order to lay blocks in straight rows, the width of the joints should be made equal to the difference between the widest block and the narrowest. (For example, if the widest block is 3½ in. and the narrowest 2¾ in., the joints should be ¾ in. wide.) If you don't want perfectly straight rows, however, you can jam the blocks together as tightly as you like.

Fill narrow joints with fine sand. For wide joints, use coarse sand or mix 4 parts sand with 1 part Portland cement. After the cement mixture is brushed into the joints, remove the excess and apply a fine spray of water. Then, after the mortar has set two or three hours, scrub the tops of the stones with a coarse damp rag

45

*A charming city terrace.
At the rear it is paved
in small cut-granite blocks
arranged in an intricate
pattern of overlapping
fans. In the foreground—a
children's play area—
brick is used because it is
kinder to young knees
and suggests that the
youngsters should not stray
beyond.*

*A tiny entrance terrace
beside the front walk
is paved in cobblestones to
contrast with the walk
and also to let water
and oxygen down to the roots
of a fine Amur maple.*

to remove mortar stains. Three days later, sprinkle with water and scrub once more with a solution of 1 part muriatic acid in 9 parts water. Get as little of the solution into the joints as possible.

Paving with Flagstones

Flagstones are large gray, blue or brown sandstones which are sold in squares, rectangles and irregular shapes. Many stock sizes of squares and rectangles are available in masonry-supply outlets, and you can have others cut to order. You can also have special shapes cut to order.

The stones make an outstanding pavement which is strong, durable, skidproof but not rough, and moderately resistant to staining. And if you use square and/or rectangular stones, the pavement is as attractive as they come. The irregular stones I usually don't like because the paving looks something like a shattered automobile windshield; but this can be minimized considerably if you don't use too many small stones.

If you use squares or rectangles of one size, you can figure the number required by calculating the square-inch or square-foot area

48

of the terrace and dividing by the square-inch or square-foot area of the stones. But if you use mixed sizes, let the masonry-supply dealer figure out what you need and give you a numbered plan showing exactly which stones go where. This adds to the total cost of the stones but will spare you the headache of arranging the stones and cutting them to fit.

For a uniform effect, be sure to tell the dealer that you want stones of the same color. Otherwise you will wind up with a mixture which may not be attractive.

The easiest way to install the stones is to lay them on a sand-and-gravel base. Follow the directions for laying concrete patio blocks. The stones should be 1½ in. thick to resist breakage.

Flagstones are also laid in mortar. But the joints stand out objectionably until they become discolored with wear and dirt. Then for some reason the mortar often begins to crack. Despite these problems, however, many terraces are paved this way.

Flagstones in squares and rectangles of assorted sizes are here used in precise rows—an unusual arrangement. Beyond is a wood deck surrounding a swimming pool.

The first step is to pour a 3-in. slab of concrete. Use the mix required for an exposed-aggregate terrace. If the terrace isn't large, the entire base can be poured in a solid sheet and struck off flush with the board forms around the edges. But for a large terrace, divide the forms into sections and pour one at a time. When completed, the top of the slab should be level but doesn't have to be smooth. Let it set overnight.

When you lay the flagstones, don't spread mortar for more than two stones at once. First, brush the base with a grout made of ½ sack Portland cement and 3 gal. water. Then trowel on a ½-in. layer of mortar made of 1 part Portland cement, 3 parts sand and enough water to give a wet but not soupy, plastic consistency.

A very formal terrace paved in irregular flagstones. Azaleas are banked against an iron railing at the front of the terrace (left).

50

Press the stones firmly but not heavily into this and check each one with a spirit level. After several are laid, lay a straightedge across them to make sure there are no high or low spots.

Allow ½-in. space between stones. Let the stones set for 24 hours before filling the joints with a 1-to-3 mortar. Pack the joints solidly and strike them off flush with the tops of the stones. Then immediately wipe off mortar and mortar stains with a damp rag. If necessary, go over the stones again in about a week with a dilute muriatic acid solution.

Paving with Kool Deck

This is a special material which is combined with white cement and marble sand and applied in a thin layer on a conventional concrete base. The finish resembles smooth coral rock or travertine.

Kool Deck's outstanding feature is the fact that it is cooler underfoot on hot, sunny days than most other pavings. For this reason, it is generally used only on terraces and walks adjacent to swimming pools. However, if your pool is close to the house, the light color of the material (there are several pastel shades) may prove objectionably glary outdoors and may also bounce too much sunlight into the house.

Although Kool Deck was developed primarily for use in hot climates, it has proved durable and useful in cold climates as well. It is skidproof and stain-resistant.

Installation must be made by a professional applicator. Make sure he has worked often with the material.

Paving with Slates

Natural-surfaced slate (the only kind to use) is another very handsome paving material. Strong and durable, it has a slight texture but is nonabrasive and therefore less skidproof than flagstone. But it is more stain-resistant. Various colors, mostly dark hues, are available. Some fade when exposed to sunlight; others do not.

Like flagstones, you can buy slates in squares, rectangles and irregular shapes. Have the dealer make a numbered layout for you if you use squares and rectangles in mixed sizes.

One-in.-thick slates can be laid on a sand-and-gravel base; but if you can afford them, 1½-in. thickness is better. Construct the terrace like one made with concrete patio blocks.

If slates are laid in mortar, follow the directions for paving with flagstones. Use ¾-in. stones.

Another large, formal terrace—this one paved in big black slates each surrounded by narrow strips of slate. The rows are laid at a 45° angle to the sides of the terrace. No mortar is used.

To keep the slates from sliding into the planting pockets, a metal curb shaped like an upside-down L has been placed around them.

Paving with Tiles

Quarry tiles, patio tiles and pavers are rugged tiles particularly suited for exterior use. They are made in squares, rectangles and a number of special shapes. Patio tiles, which are as much as 1 ft. square, are a brownish red. Quarry tiles and pavers are smaller and come in just about any color you may want. There are also units with special designs and textures.

Tiles are more colorful and more stain-resistant than other paving materials, and also the easiest to clean. But they are more breakable than most materials and slippery when wet.

You can lay tiles in a sand-and-gravel base if they are at least 9 in. square and ¾ in. thick. Smaller tiles shift around too much. Follow the directions for installing concrete patio blocks.

The best way to lay tiles, however, is in concrete because they are much more durable and stay put. But to do this properly, you should be a professional tile setter who knows and follows the installation procedures spelled out in the handbook published by the Tile Council of America.

Ceramic tiles in octagons and squares make a handsome floor for this partially enclosed terrace.

**Paving with
Wood Blocks**

When wet, wood blocks are as slippery as banana peels; but at other times, they are far and away the pleasantest material to walk on because they are very resilient, quiet and nonglary. They also blend beautifully into the landscape when weathered.

On the other hand, they have a short life and are hard to keep clean because they stain easily and dirt becomes embedded in them.

*Square wood blocks
make this circular terrace
pleasantly quiet and
resilient underfoot.
But it's slippery when wet.*

Redwood and cypress are the best "natural" woods for a terrace paving. Then comes red cedar. But you can use any wood if you have it pressure-treated at the mill with a wood preservative.

There is no standard-size wood paving block. Anything measuring 4 x 4 in. on the surface and at least 4 in. deep will do. Squares or rectangles are much preferred because they can be placed so close together that they are, in effect, locked into the terrace. If you use rounds, the wide spaces between them must be filled—preferably with concrete, which rather spoils the beauty of the wood.

Lay the blocks like bricks on a sand-and-gravel base. The end grain should be exposed. Either set the edging blocks in concrete

Because this very informal terrace is not expected to get much use except for occasional sunbathing, it is paved with big slabs cut from tree trunks which are interplanted with a tiny ground cover.

or use deep blocks and set them on end. The alternative is to surround the terrace with a deep curb of metal or boards.

It should not be necessary to sweep sand into the joints if you lay the blocks together tightly.

Paving with a Combination of Materials

Most people do this for the decorative effect. But as pointed out in the earlier description of my large terrace, you can also combine materials to create a distinction between different terrace areas. Whatever your purpose, be restrained in your design. Indoors you can go wild (if you have good design sense). But your terrace should be compatible with nature, which is restrained. Furthermore, it's the world surrounding your terrace that makes the terrace attractive, not the paving.

A circular terrace paved with dry-laid bricks and square concrete patio blocks set in at random. Small plants are tucked into crevices and pockets in the floor, and the entire terrace is planted around with several kinds of rhododendron, leucothoe and other choice plants.

Carpeting the Terrace

Carpeting a screened or otherwise closed-in porch is one thing. You expect carpet indoors and a porch of this type has the feeling of being indoors. But to carpet an open terrace or deck—I personally can't buy it though I know it is done.

Despite claims, indoor-outdoor carpet simply isn't made for use outdoors. True, it's comfortable to walk on and play on, and initially it may be pretty. But it gets dirty and shows stains, and no matter how much vacuuming and hosing and scrubbing you do, it's never really clean and bright. When wet, it's soggy and nasty-feeling and takes a long time to dry. Last but not least, it has to be replaced about every ten years.

If you insist on using the stuff, buy an acrylic carpet because it is more durable than polypropylene. Installation is usually made over a concrete slab.

Removing Stains from Terrace Floors

The secret in all cases is to get at them as soon as possible.

OIL AND GREASE   Squirt undiluted dishwashing or household detergent on the stain, scrub it in and let it stand for ten minutes. Then scrub with boiling water and rinse. A repeat treatment may be necessary.

PAINT   Scrape off what you can with a knife, then apply a liquid paint remover to soften the rest. Rinse with water if the paint remover is of the water-wash type; with paint thinner otherwise.

Powdered cleaners made especially for use on floors of commercial garages are excellent for paint as well as grease. Follow the directions on the package.

CRAYON   Scrub with boiling water.

SMOKE   Scrub with an abrasive cleanser.

RUST   Scrub with a phosphoric acid cleaner and a bristle brush. Rinse thoroughly.

EFFLORESCENCE   This is the powdery white salt which often appears on masonry. Remove with a bristle brush and wash with 1 part muriatic acid in 9 parts water.

5 Walls and Roofs for the Terrace

There are several reasons for building walls around a terrace:

To raise the level of the terrace.

To keep people from falling off a raised terrace.

To define the terrace, making it clearly separate from the lawn and garden.

To give the terrace privacy.

To protect against the wind.

To serve as a seat.

Whatever the purpose, all masonry walls are built in the same way. (Wood walls, or fences, are something else again, of course.) But different rules apply to their design.

1. If a wall is built to raise the terrace, it is a retaining wall, and the fill poured behind it is constantly exerting pressure against it. Consequently, you should not build a concrete masonry wall more than 3 ft. high—that is, 3 ft. from the ground up to the top of the terrace floor.

If the wall is more than 3 ft. high, it should be much more massive than the walls described below, and should be built by a competent mason.

2. If a dry wall—a wall built without mortar—is used as a retaining wall, it should be no more than 18 in. high. One foot is safer.

3. The walls described below should not exceed 4 ft. in height above the level of the terrace floor. If you go higher, you must reinforce the wall with steel or add to its thickness to hold it upright against winds.

Note that a 4-ft. wall can be built atop a 3-ft. retaining wall.

4. To protect people against falls, raised terraces should be surrounded by walls (or fences or benches) rising 30 in. or more above the terrace floor. This is the minimum "safe" height. But you can keep the wall as low as 18 in. if you recognize that it isn't safe.

You can omit walls around a raised terrace only if the terrace is just a foot higher than the surrounding ground and some sort of definite visual barrier is provided between the edges of the

terrace floor and the retaining walls. On the terrace illustrated on this page, for example, an 18-in.-wide bed of English ivy warns people away from the walls built to raise the level of the terrace.

Building Brick Walls

The first step in building a brick wall is to dig a trench and construct a footing which will hold the wall upright in spite of wind, moisture and frost. The bottom of the trench should be at least 18 in. below ground level in warm climates, and should be below the frost line in cold climates. Place two rows of greased boards on opposite sides of the trench to serve as forms. The boards should be 8 in. high and spaced 16 in. apart. Brace them well and make sure they're level. Then pour in concrete, spade it thoroughly to eliminate entrapped air, and strike it off flush with the top of the forms. Buy ready-mixed concrete delivered by truck. If you prefer to mix your own, the proportions should be 1 sack Portland cement, 2¼ cu. ft. sand and 4 cu. ft. coarse aggregate up to 1½ in. diameter. Allow the footing to set about 24 hours before building on it.

Lay the bricks two tiers thick to give a total wall thickness of 8 in. The simplest pattern is a running bond in which the vertical joints in one stretcher course fall in the middle of the bricks in the adjoining stretcher courses. The entire wall can be made with stretcher courses, or you can alternate five stretcher courses and then one header course. (In a stretcher course, the bricks are laid lengthwise of the wall; in a header course, they are laid across the wall.) All joints should be ½ in. thick. For mortar, mix 1 part

59

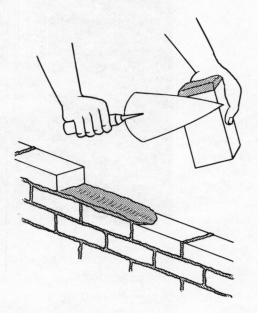

Constructing a brick wall. After a furrowed ribbon of concrete is spread over the preceding course, butter the end of the brick you are laying and set it firmly into place.

masonry cement with 3 parts sand and enough water to make a plastic but not soupy mixture.

Build the wall to a taut string marking the front of the wall. At the start, tie the string to stakes driven into the ground; but as the wall rises, tie the string around the end bricks.

Build the wall from the ends and work toward the middle. Until you reach the top of the wall, the ends are always built up two or three courses above those in between. Check the wall continually with a carpenter's level to make sure it is flat from end to end and front to back.

Bricklaying technique is simple but you must work at the job a while before you master it.

First wet the bricks thoroughly with water. Soaking for an hour is the best procedure.

Spread a ribbon of mortar—first on the footing and then on the wall—which is one brick wide and no more than two or three bricks long. Then make a slight furrow down the center of the ribbon with the point of your mason's trowel.

Put a large dab of mortar on the end of the brick you are laying. This is called buttering. Then press the brick squarely into the ribbon of mortar and with the buttered end against the end of the brick previously laid. Don't twist the brick into the mortar. Tap it down firmly with your trowel, and scrape off the excess mortar.

When the mortar has set to some extent, finish the joint to

60

make it smooth. The easiest tool to use is a piece of pipe a little wider than the joint. Draw it along the joint to give a concave profile. If you get mortar stains on the bricks, wipe them off with a damp cloth. Then about two weeks later, scrub off any stains that remain with a solution of 1 part muriatic acid in 9 parts water. Since the acid etches concrete, keep it out of the joints as much as possible.

Don't let too much time go by before laying bricks in a mortar ribbon. If the mortar loses much moisture before you get the bricks down, toss it back into the mortar box and mix well.

If after you lay a brick you find it needs to be reset, scrape up the mortar, return it to the box, and start over again with fresh mortar. The mortar you mix originally is usable for no more than 2½ hours if the temperature is over 80°; 3½ hours if under 80°. However, if it gets stiff during this period, you can add a little water to it.

The vertical joint between tiers is filled by slushing mortar into it. Work your trowel up and down to eliminate air. But except for the last bricks laid in the middle of a row, never make the end joints this way because they are not as strong as those made by buttering the bricks.

When building a corner, construct the walls on both sides of the corner at the same time (but complete one wall from end to end before tackling the other). The bricks right at the corner interlock. That is, the corner brick in the first course runs lengthwise of, say, the front wall; that in the second course runs lengthwise of the side wall; and so on, alternating, to the top.

Eight-foot brick wall of unusual design. Succulents planted on a mammoth piece of driftwood are here being misted with water.

**Building
Concrete-block Walls**

If you can build a brick wall, you can build one of concrete blocks, and vice versa. The procedure is very similar.

Standard blocks have nominal dimensions of 8 x 8 x 16 in. (The actual dimensions are 7⅝ x 7⅝ x 15⅝ in., thus allowing for joints ⅜ in. wide.) Before ordering blocks, lay out the wall on graph paper to an exact multiple of 16 in. long. This will eliminate the necessity for cutting blocks and will also simplify ordering. If

Pierced concrete block wall is as handsome from the neighbor's side as from the terrace on the far side. The height of the wall—less than 4 ft.— bespeaks good neighbors.

you use a running bond (the strongest), it will be apparent from the sketch that you need several types of blocks: full-length stretchers with deep hollows in the ends; full-length corner blocks with one end square and the other hollow; half-length corner blocks with one end square and the other hollow; and 4-in.-thick solid blocks to cap the wall.

Build the wall up on a poured-concrete footing 8 in. high and 16 in. wide. Work from the ends of the wall toward the middle and use a taut cord to keep it straight. If building a corner, construct the wall on both sides and interlock the corner blocks. Check your work regularly with a carpenter's level.

Put down a mortar bed for only one block at a time. The bed actually consists of two ribbons of mortar on the front and back edges of the blocks in the course below. Do not put mortar on the cross strips. Then butter one end of the block you are laying, and set it into place on the mortar bed and against the end of the previous block. Tap it firmly into place; scrape off the excess mortar and return it to the mortar box; and after the joints have set, tool them with a piece of pipe.

Attractive pierced concrete block wall serves as a background for carefully selected vines and shrubs, including the big-leaved schefflera in the corner.

About four or five days after the wall is completed, you can paint it with a couple of coats of exterior latex paint.

Many ornamental concrete blocks are on the market. Sizes are variable. Some blocks made to resemble large bricks or cut stones might be substituted for standard blocks in a retaining wall. But the more ornamental blocks are strictly for aboveground use to give privacy or protection from the wind or simply to serve as a decorative background. Some of these blocks have designs molded into the face; others are pierced to permit construction of a grille-type wall; still others are coated with a colorful glaze. Despite these differences, all are used in a wall like standard blocks.

Building a Stone Wall with Mortar

The construction principles for a stone wall are the same as those for a brick wall; but be prepared to spend much more time on the job, because it's a lot like putting a jigsaw puzzle together.

Where I live today, stone-wall building is comparatively easy because many of the ledge rocks are striated, so all you have to do is trim up the edges of the stones a bit and stack one flat on top of the other. But where I used to live, the ledges were solid and the fieldstones of every conceivable shape and size; so unless you had a load of stone shipped in from some other part of the country, wall building was a slow, tricky and fascinating try-this-try-that undertaking. (Yes, you can cut stones with a cold chisel and hammer; but only certain kinds respond amiably to your efforts.)

Because you're working with irregular shapes and sizes, you can't build a stone wall less than 1 ft. thick, and you will undoubtedly save work if you make it 18 to 24 in. Build it up from a footing about 2 ft. wide and a foot deep. Unless you have nice rectangular stones, there's no need to give the footing a smooth top; so you can make it of stones you don't want, with concrete slushed down around them.

If building a retaining wall, work to a string stretched along the outside of the wall. But if building an aboveground wall which will be seen from both sides, use two parallel strings. Since the surfaces of a stone wall are irregular, tie the strings to stakes, not around the ends of the wall. This means that there's no need to work from the ends of the wall toward the middle, though it's an easy method of operation.

Be sure the stones are free of soil and other matter before using them. For mortar, use 1 part Portland cement with 3 parts sand. The joints must be at least ½ in. wide, but many will exceed this.

Before embedding a stone in mortar, try it dry to make sure it fits, looks well, and won't fall out or sag while the mortar is setting. Some stones will fit best if laid the length of the wall; some will fit best across the wall. Years ago when I built a large stone terrace and was hard up for good stones, I even set occasional flat stones on edge to make them look important.

Place a mortar bed for one stone at a time. If possible, butter the end of the stone before setting it in position. But if you can't do this because of the shape of the stone or of the previous stone,

64

you can't. Frequently the only way to surround a stone with mortar is to slush it down around the ends and back; and to keep it in place while doing this, you may have to hold a hand against the front of the joint.

In a retaining wall, the back can be uneven and crude; but fill the joints well to keep out as much moisture as possible. In an aboveground wall, if good stones are difficult to come by, use the best on the front and back and fill in between them with rubble and mortar.

Building Dry Stone Walls

Although I can become lyrical about the beauty of an old New England stone wall, I don't think I have ever seen an aboveground dry wall surrounding a terrace anywhere. But a dry wall makes a good low retaining wall because moisture in the ground behind it can escape through it, and because you can grow pretty little flowers, vines and ground covers in the chinks of the wall.

To build such a wall, however, you should have stones which are reasonably flat and rather large. If they are really flat—so they can be stacked pretty much like bricks—a wall need not be much more than 12 in. from front to back. But if the stones are not so flat, the wall should be 18 in. minimum from front to back.

In warm climates, dig a trench 1 ft. deep; in cold, make it 18 to 24 in. deep. It should be at least 1 ft. wider than the wall. Fill it with rocks and rubble to form a footing for the wall. Don't just throw these in; fit them fairly carefully so they create a firm base. Concrete is not required.

Center the wall on the footing. If possible, tip the stones backward slightly; don't let them tip forward. Wedging stone shims between large stones to prevent wobbling is perfectly legal, though the old Yankee wall builders never had to resort to this practice. To stabilize the wall, don't build up one stone directly over another; lap it over two stones instead. And don't allow vertical joints in adjacent courses to line up.

Building Fences

Whereas walls around terraces are generally—but not always—low, fences are almost always high to provide privacy and/or to fend off the wind. Six-ft. fences are common; 8-ft., not unknown.

Unfortunately, most homeowners build and maintain fences badly. In the pretty little town of Carmel, California, for example, about every other house has a fence; and eight out of ten of the fences are in a woeful state of disrepair. Even those in good repair are all too often unattractive.

Probably the most important job in fence building is to get the posts vertical, in a straight line and solidly set. Use cords stretched between stakes to position and align the holes. The normal spacing between posts is 8 ft. center to center; but in a very windy location, you might use a 6-ft. spacing; and in a very protected location you might use 10. In any case, start at one end of the fence and mark the center of each successive posthole with a stake.

If you live on a hillside, before locating the postholes, you must decide whether the top of the fence will follow the contours of the land or will be in level steps. Generally, on a very slight slope or in open country or if you're building a low, open rail or picket fence or the like, the fence follows the slope. But as I just said, most terrace fences are high, and they are also pretty solid-looking, so they are usually stepped. These also conform better with the walls of the house. To locate the postholes for such a fence, establish the first one at the top of the slope and pull the string out *level*—not

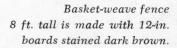

Basket-weave fence 8 ft. tall is made with 12-in. boards stained dark brown.

A high fence on sloping ground usually looks best when it is stepped down the hill, as here. Though it's within a few feet of the street, the terrace behind the fence has excellent privacy.

parallel with the slope. Measure the spacing between posts along the string, and drop a plumb line to the ground at each location.

You can dig postholes with a shovel, but a posthole digger is better because you can work faster and because it makes a narrow, straight hole with solid sides which help to keep the post from wobbling. If you must dig a lot of holes, however, rent a power-driven auger.

Though it takes time, make the holes at least 30 in. deep. This will help to hold the fence upright even when it is buffeted by winds or run into. Pour a couple of inches of gravel in the bottom to allow water to drain away from the posts. In dense clay soil use 6 in. Tamp well. Then, after cutting the posts to the proper height (this is hard to do after the fence is built), set the posts, and pour several more inches of gravel around them.

In most situations it is perfectly satisfactory to fill the holes to the top with the soil and stones you dug out. Pour in a few inches at a time and tamp heavily with a 2 x 4. At the top, slope the soil away from the posts.

In windy or street-side locations, however, set the posts in concrete. This is particularly important if the fence is solid or unusually high. Use the same concrete mixture as for a footing under a wall.

First surround the bottom of the posts with several inches of gravel. Then pour in concrete and pack it down well. If there is only an inch or two of space between a post and the sides of the hole, widen the hole for about a foot down from the top to provide a heavier concrete base.

If you intend to put in a planting bed under the fence, don't bring the concrete all the way up to ground level. But if the fence will be in grass, concrete at ground level will eliminate the need for hand-clipping grass around the posts. In either case, slope the concrete slightly away from the posts.

When setting posts, make sure they are straight up and down and in line. To do this, set the end posts first, plumb them carefully with a carpenter's level or plumb line before starting to fill in around them, and plumb them several times as filling proceeds. Then stretch cords between the posts at the top and about a foot above the ground. Nail the cords to the sides of the posts. Then, as you set the intermediate posts, make sure they just touch the cords; and use a level or plumb line to make sure they don't lean toward either of the end posts.

Posts for a terrace fence are generally made of 4 x 4s. Use redwood, cypress, red cedar or any other wood which has been impregnated—preferably at a mill—with wood preservative. Heartwood is better than sapwood because it is more resistant to decay.

Because of its high visibility, the design of a fence is as important as its construction. One of the first points to be considered, if it is close to a lot line, is how your neighbor is going to like it, because the backs of fences are rarely as pretty as the fronts. Many, in fact, are downright ugly. Simply in the interest of neighborhood harmony, do try to avoid a design that will give offense. A few neat posts and rails are acceptable; but when you add a network of braces, watch out. The ideal, of course, is a fence that looks the same on both sides.

Also in the interest of neighborhood harmony, it's advisable not to place a fence exactly on a lot line. Pull it in far enough so you can get behind it to paint or otherwise maintain it without being accused of trespassing.

A second obvious point to think about when designing a fence is what you want the fence to do. If its main purpose is to provide privacy, a solid fence or one that appears solid is needed. But if you're trying to screen out the wind, a somewhat open fence is

Tiny terrace is shielded
from the neighboring house
only a few feet away by
a stockade fence and
rolls of woven reeds
which are extended over the
terrace to keep off the
sun. The reeds on the roof
are supported in 1 x 2-in.
wood strips laid across the
rafters. You can support
them just as well at less
cost by substituting wires for
the strips.

called for if the terrace does not have a solid roof. Why? Because when wind approaches a solid fence, it veers upward over it and comes right down on the other side. It's like a high hurdler. When it comes to a fence with openings, it blasts straight ahead; but in passing through the openings, it is broken up and comes out on the lee side as a whisper.

(On a terrace with a solid roof, either type of fence can be used. One with openings admits a gentle breeze; a solid fence does not.)

An open-and-shut case. Louvers cut from 2 x 4s are pivoted so they can be opened by hand to any desired degree for air circulation, closed tight for privacy. Or you can open some of the panels in the fence while keeping others closed.

There are very few prefabricated fences which deserve any prizes for beauty. Most tend to be a little cute or flimsy. Sears, for instance, has a good solid board fence which it has spoiled by rounding the tops of the boards. It also has a delicate-looking basket-weave which is a far cry from the sturdy homemade design shown on page 66. As for the popular stockade fence which every lumber yard sells, just what in the world is pretty about it or makes it appropriate to a terrace behind a residence in a civilized world?

Several good designs for terrace fences are illustrated, and there are others. Just don't get carried away with trying to be unusual, because a large fence is best used as a background for plants, not as an important ornamental feature itself.

The materials used in the fence must, of course, be selected for practicality as well as appearance.

Wood should have natural resistance to decay or should be treated with a wood preservative. This is especially important in the case of posts, rails and other horizontal members on which

70

Porch in a closely built community is shielded from the sun and neighbors by a wall of horizontal wood louvers. The louvers also guard against strong winds but permit a constant movement of air into and off the porch.

A very high louvered fence built to shield the terrace from a nearby house up the hill. The fence rails are made of 2 x 4s; the louvers of 6-in. boards set at a 45° angle.

Mail-order-house
version of a basket-weave
fence. The entire terrace is
ringed by well-tended
shrubs and perennials.

Simple painted fence
with V joints is always
handsome and takes on
added interest when sun
slanting through the
roof grid strikes it.

water may stand. Don't forget, however, that vertical members nailed to the sides of rails are often rotted out by moisture getting in between them and the rails.

If allowed to weather naturally, most woods in time acquire a pleasant patina; but whether this is even depends on how much different areas are exposed to sun and rain. For an even natural finish, apply a bleaching oil. If you prefer the appearance of new wood, however, apply a water repellent. On the other hand, if you want to color the fence without painting it, use a penetrating oil stain.

Plywood used for fence panels must be an exterior grade. You can finish it with any of the materials just mentioned. Other excellent materials for solid panels are asbestos-cement board and hardboard. Both can be left natural or painted. Hardboard panels are available in various tough, paintlike factory finishes.

Polyester reinforced with fiberglass is the most durable and colorfast of the plastic panels.

If decorative perforated panels are used in a fence, they should be made of aluminum or hardboard. But the most beautiful of the perforated materials are sculptured wood and plastics.

Nails must be of rust-resistant galvanized steel or aluminum. Screws and bolts should be galvanized, aluminum, brass or bronze.

Building a curving fence is trickier than building a straight one.

The degree of the curve depends on what is most suitable for the terrace and depends also on the dimensions of the timbers from which you cut the fence rails. For example, if the curve has

Railing on a raised terrace overlooking gardens, swimming pool and ocean is specially designed and built of steel.

a radius of about 8 ft., the rails can be cut most economically from 6-ft. lengths of 2 x 12. On the other hand, if the curve has a radius of about 10 ft., the rails should be cut from 8-ft. lengths of 2 x 12; while if the curve has a radius of about 3½ ft., the rails should be cut from 4-ft. lengths of 2 x 12.

To fabricate the rails, draw the desired curve on a 2 x 12 or other wide timber, and then cut out the rail with a saber saw. Use this as a pattern for the other rails.

After drawing the curve on the ground with a "compass" made out of a length of string and a couple of spikes tied to the ends, establish the position of the first post. Then lay the rails on the ground to establish the positions of the other posts.

If palings are nailed to the front of the fence, they should be made of 1 x 2 or 1 x 3-in. boards. Vertical louvers nailed between the top and bottom rails, however, can be made of the same boards used in a straight louvered fence. If you want a fence with solid panels, use asbestos-cement board or hardboard, both of which are easily bent. Some plastic panels are also bendable.

Installing Sliding Glass Doors in the House Wall

Unless you have done a great deal of carpentry work and understand how a house is constructed, installing large glass doors (and picture windows) is not for you. But by all means take an interest in the doors you have put in.

1. Be sure they are made with safety glass.

2. Regardless of the climate, the glass should be double-paned to keep out cold and heat.

3. If the doors face west or an open terrace to the south, you may find it advisable to specify tinted glass to reduce the glare indoors. (Brown is the best color because it distorts nature's colors least.)

4. Buy a top-quality door: there is less chance that water and air can leak in under it.

5. In a very cold climate, buy a door with wood frames: it costs more than a door with aluminum frames but the frames do not transmit cold to the same extent.

Building a Roof to Keep Off the Rain

It's a shame not to roof at least part of your terrace so you can enjoy it in wet weather. And I do mean *enjoy* it. Sitting on a terrace on a warm summer night as the rain falls is an entirely different experience from that usually associated with terrace life. The rain patters a lullaby on the roof. Lightning flickers across the

74

distant sky. The grass and vegetation glisten in the light splashing from the house windows. And the warm earth gives off a faintly sweet smell.

A roof is also important on chill autumn nights, because it holds in heat and makes the terrace livable when the world beyond is too cool for comfort.

Building a roof over a terrace distant from the house is a job best left to a carpenter. But there's no reason why you cannot build one over a terrace adjoining the house.

A shed roof is the simplest. The degree of pitch depends on the roofing material used. If you choose asphalt shingles to match the house roof, the pitch should be 4 in. in 1 ft. For wood shingles, it should be 3 in. in 1 ft. Asphalt roll roofing, corrugated plastic and metal require a pitch of 2 in. in 1 ft.

The method of framing the roof is the same for all roofing materials, but the size and spacing of the timbers varies somewhat according to the weight of the roof.

At the back of the terrace, the roof is supported on a horizontal 2 x 4-in. ledger strip attached to the house wall. Nail the strip through the siding into the studs with 6-in. galvanized-steel spikes. Drive two spikes into every stud. The height of the ledger strip depends on the pitch and depth of the roof. At its lowest point—which is the front edge—the roof should be at least 8 ft. high, but it can be dropped 6 in. This means that if the front edge of the roof is 10 ft. out from the house and the roof has a 3-in. pitch, the top of the ledger strip should be 10½ ft. above the terrace floor. For a roof with a 2-in. pitch, the height of the ledger strip would be 9 ft. 8 in.

At the front of the terrace, the roof is supported on 4 x 4-in. posts of redwood, cypress, red cedar or other wood treated with preservative. If the terrace paving is set in sand, sink the ends of the posts into the ground 3 ft. to prevent lateral movement and also to tie down the roof so the wind can't blow it off. Firming the soil around the posts should hold them; but if the soil is very porous, it's well to surround the posts with concrete.

If the terrace floor is made of exposed-aggregate concrete or built on a concrete slab, anchor the posts to the top of the slab. There are various special devices for doing this, or you can use large angle irons and fasten them to the pavement with screws driven into lead anchors.

Except for plastic roofing, the posts should be no more than

*In the tropical climate of
Hawaii, terraces grow
big and roofs are essential to
keep off sun and rain.
Massive timbers are
required to anchor the roof
against strong ocean
winds.*

10 ft. apart across the front of the terrace; and they should be no more than 10 ft. from the house wall. If the roof is much deeper than this, additional posts are needed along the sides of the terrace. For plastic roofing, the minimum corresponding spacings are 12 ft.

The front posts are tied together by a beam. For a plastic roof, use a 2 x 6 and notch it into the upper ends of the posts. Secure it with bolts. For any other roof, use a 4 x 4 and rest it on top of the posts. Attach it with galvanized post caps which are bolted over the ends of the posts and to the sides of the beam.

The length of the beam equals the distance from one end post to the other. To this you can add 1 ft. overhang at each end for a heavy roof; as much as 2 ft. for a plastic roof.

If the house siding is wood shingles or beveled boards, it's a good idea before putting up the rafters to install a 12-in. flashing strip which will seal the joint between the siding and the terrace roof. (A flat strip is used for most roofing; but a special strip with corrugations along one edge is used on roofs covered with corrugated material.) Push the strip up under the butts of the shingles or boards which will be just above the roof when completed. Bend the lower edge outward. It will be attached to the roof later. (If the house has any other kind of siding, the flashing is usually installed after the roof is completed.)

The rafters are cut from 2 x 6-in. timbers and are installed perpendicular to the house. For a heavy roof, place them on top of the ledger strip and beam, and a toenail them in place with 4- or 5-in. galvanized nails. Space the rafters 16 or 24 in. apart.

Framing for a porch roof.

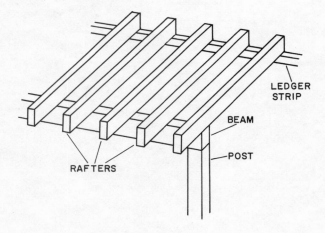

LEDGER STRIP

BEAM

POST

RAFTERS

Terrace tucked into a corner
of the house is partially
covered with a
flat roof supported on lacy
ironwork.

This rustic terrace in
Brown County, Indiana, is
built some distance
from the house to take in a
view. The roof is covered
with cedar shakes.

For a plastic roof, hang the rafters on the side of the ledger strip with stirrup-like metal hangers. If you use the popular 26-in.-wide panels, space the rafters 24 in. apart. For larger panels, the space between rafters should equal the panel width minus 2 in., and 2 x 6-in. cross braces should be nailed between the rafters under the lower end of the panels and midway between the two ends. Similar cross bracing is needed for 26-in. panels only if over 10 ft. long.

For a heavy roof, you can allow a 2-ft. overhang beyond the beam; for a plastic roof, 3 ft. Nail a 2 x 6 across the lower ends of the rafters to tie them together and to serve as a nailing base for the roof deck or plastic panels.

The deck for a roof covered with asphalt or cedar shingles or metal is made of ¾-in. exterior-grade plywood or 6- or 8-in. boards. Because the underside of the deck is usually exposed, the underside of the plywood should be free of knots and voids. To prevent the points of nails coming through, use 1-in. galvanized roofing nails for both types of shingles. (The first course of asphalt shingles should be fastened down with asphalt roofing cement rather than nails.) Metal sheets are put down with 1¾-in. nails driven through the deck into the rafters. Use aluminum nails for aluminum roofing; galvanized for steel roofing.

Asphalt roofing must be laid over a 1-in. thickness of plywood to keep the nails from showing through underneath.

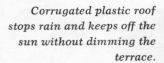

Corrugated plastic roof stops rain and keeps off the sun without dimming the terrace.

A domed plastic roof protects and warms part of the eating deck shown on page 3.

Directions for installing these four types of roofing are given in so many books, publications and manufacturers' leaflets that I skip them here. Fiberglass-reinforced plastic panels are laid directly over rafters. Overlap adjacent panels 1½ in. and seal the joints with the caulking compound supplied by the roofing dealer. The open edge of the lap should point away from the prevailing wind.

Drill holes through the plastic panels; and then fasten the panels to the rafters with aluminum or galvanized screw nails with neoprene washers under the heads. On the vertical edges, space the nails 1 ft. apart. On the horizontal edges, at the ledger strip and over the fascia board, use at least three nails per panel.

Regardless of the roofing material used, the last step in building a roof is to flash the joint at the house wall. If the flashing strip is already in place, just bend it down tight to the roof and anchor it with asphalt roofing cement or, in the case of a plastic roof, with the same caulking used to seal joints. If the flashing strip is not in place because you could not force it up under the siding, it must be nailed to the face of the siding and then bent down over the roof. To make the top edge waterproof, squeeze a heavy ribbon of poly-sulfide rubber or silicone caulking compound between it and the house wall.

81

**Building a Roof to
Filter the Sun**

Understandably enough, sunshades are more widely used in dry, hot climates than in cooler, damp ones. But they are useful wherever the sun makes life miserable on a terrace and there are no trees to give protection. Here are four relatively simple ways to build them:

LATH ROOF   This takes little skill to construct and the final product is attractive and highly efficient.

The laths are actually 1 x 2-in. boards installed in parallel rows 1 in. apart for deep shade, 2 in. apart for half shade. They can be laid in any direction; but generally a north-south axis is preferred because it yields an ever-changing pattern of sun and shade on the terrace as the sun moves from east to west. The entire roof can be flat or pitched.

If the laths are laid perpendicular to the house, you shouldn't try to roof a terrace more than 16 ft. long; otherwise, you may wind up with posts in the center. Nail a 2 x 4-in. ledger strip to the house wall and erect two posts topped with a beam at the front edge of the terrace. The posts can be spaced as much as 12 ft. apart if you use a 4 x 4 for the beam. The beam can extend 2 ft. beyond the posts at either end (thus making a 16-ft.-long roof).

Unless the terrace is very shallow, additional posts and beams will be needed between the house and terrace edge. In a mild climate, the maximum spacing between the front and intermediate post and the intermediate post and the wall should be 8 ft. In a climate with heavy snow, reduce the spacing to 6 ft. to give added strength to the laths.

Lay the laths across the beams and ledger strips and secure them with galvanized-steel nails. You can let them overhang the beam at the front edge of the terrace as much as 1 ft.

Running laths parallel with the wall of the house permits you to roof a terrace of any length without erecting posts in the middle. However, the 4 x 4-in. posts along the front edge of the terrace should be no more than 12 ft. from the house wall.

Nail a ledger strip to the house wall 4 in. higher than the tops of the posts. Attach 4 x 4-in. beams to the side of the ledger with metal hangers, and attach them to the tops of the posts with steel post caps. The space between the beams (and posts) should be no more than 8 ft. in a mild climate; 6 ft. in a snowy climate.

The shadow pattern on the terrace floor in the foreground shows what happens when a terrace has a lath sunshade.

The beams can overhang the posts as much as 2 ft., and the laths can overhang the end beams 1 ft.

WOVEN-REED ROOF   This type of roof is covered with rolls of slender reeds or bamboo strips woven tightly together to produce a thin matting. Although the shade provided is complete, it does not seem oppressive because narrow, irregular lines of light show through between the reeds.

Since a roll which covers a 6 x 15-ft. area costs only about $10, the total cost of roofing a terrace is low. But the rolls have a relatively short life and may be badly buffeted by wind. And they should usually be taken down every fall.

The supporting framework includes a 2 x 4-in. ledger strip, 4 x 4-in. posts and beam, and 2 x 4-in. rafters perpendicular to the house. Because the reeds are very lightweight, the posts can be spaced up to 16 ft. apart but should be within 12 ft. of the house wall. Space the rafters 8 ft. apart and attach them to the sides of the ledger strip and beam with metal hangers.

Stretch 18-gauge galvanized steel wires the length of the roof and fasten them securely to the tops of the rafters. Use three wires for each 6-ft.-wide roll and place them close to the edges of the roll and in the middle. Roll the reeds out over these. Then place 1-in.square strips of wood on the roof directly above the wires, and fasten them through the reeds to the wires to keep the rolls flat and secure.

LOUVERED ROOF   The louvered roof is excellent for a terrace facing almost due south, because the louvers running east and west block the high rays of the sun but admit ample light.

The framework consists of 2 x 6-in. beams notched into posts at the front edge of the terrace and extending from the posts back to the house at the ends of the terrace, thus forming a large rectangle. Space the posts up to 12 ft. apart and 12 ft. out from the house wall.

From a 2 x 6-in. ledger strip on the house to the front beams run a series of 2 x 6-in. "rafters" which divide the rectangle into equal-size rectangles no more than 6 ft. wide. Hang the "rafters" from the sides of the beam and the ledger strip.

Make the louvers of 8-in. boards cut to fit between the "rafters," and toenail them to the sides of the "rafters" at an angle of 45°. The angle should be away from the sun; that is, the bottom edges of the boards are farther south than the top edges. If you space the louvers 1 ft. apart, they will admit some sunlight at noon but little or none at other times of the day. Yet as you sit on the terrace, you can look straight up and see the sky in 6-in. strips.

You can reduce this spacing, however, if you wish to screen out more sun and light.

Terrace on a rocky Massachusetts coast has an upswept louvered roof supported on two-story-high columns.

A form of egg-crate roof with the openings shaped in long rectangles. A silent pool is wrapped around the corner (foreground).

EGG-CRATE ROOF   This is much less effective than a louvered roof at noontime but is of considerable value as a sunshade on east and west terraces.

Form a large rectangle as for a louvered roof, but use 2 x 8s for the beams and ledger strip. Then with 8-in. boards divide the rectangle into smaller squares with perpendicular sides. The size of the squares or rectangles depends on what you think looks best. Eighteen-in. squares are a good average. Rectangles run from 12 to 18 in. wide and up to about 4 ft. long. If building rectangles, they should be on an east-west axis to provide greater protection against the noonday sun.

This terrace faces almost due west because that's where the view is— and who could pass it up? A large canvas awning cuts off most of the sun, and a maple has been planted to give further protection in the future.

Awnings for a Terrace

Awnings will always be favorite covers for terraces despite the fact that they fade, wear out and become discolored, and must be put up in the spring and taken down in the fall. I guess people like them because they're attractive and give protection against both sun and rain, yet let a certain amount of light through.

But don't try to make your own awnings. Let someone who knows how, design what you need and erect the framework for it.

6 Heating and Cooling the Terrace

The first house Elizabeth and I owned had three terraces, but only the one off the dining room really stands out in our memories. It was gorgeous even though it did face the setting sun. It was long and perhaps half as wide, and was completely covered by a low, almost flat roof supported on enormous hand-hewn timbers. The end wall opposite the dining room was built of fieldstone and just the right height for sitting. The back wall was also stone but rose to within 2 ft. of the roof structure. Whenever a breeze stirred, the heat building up under the roof was wiped out through the opening and we were comfortable.

But we enjoyed the terrace most in the evening—not just warm evenings but also when the temperature fell. I recall one night when we gave a large party for our teen-age daughters. It was early June but the weather was raw, and since we had no intention of turning the house over to a gang of youngsters, I constructed a brick platform on the lawn just off the terrace and kept a log fire roaring. The kids were delighted.

On another evening when we were entertaining our own friends, the temperature plummeted with the setting sun. So I dragged the barbecue grill onto the terrace and built a charcoal fire in it. And again everyone was happy.

I am not sure whether, on either occasion, people actually were warm or merely thought they were. But if you suddenly need a little heat on your terrace, I recommend my emergency measures.

But a permanent heating system is better, of course.

The first requirement is a solid roof. It prevents the rapid dissipation of heat that builds up in the general confines of the terrace during the day. And it also holds in the heat that the heating system provides.

The second requirement—on some terraces, anyway—is a wind screen. This can be constructed in three ways:

1. If you don't have a view, you can build a fence like those discussed in the preceding chapter. On a roofed terrace, build a solid fence if you want to shut off the wind entirely; or a fence with openings if you want a gentle breeze. On an open terrace, however, a fence with openings is best.

2. If you have a view, you need a transparent fence which lets in the view while warding off the wind. Your choice of design is limited. Whether the terrace is roofed or not, the fence must be solid. You can build it of large sheets of plate glass or clear plastic centered in a simple timber frame. Or you can build a large "picture window" with small panes of sheet glass.

Almost breathtaking terrace in Washington is a full story down from the main floor of the old house. This is the scene that greets you in the spring when you step out onto the stairway leading down. The entire terrace is surrounded by high walls and is paved in pink bricks laid in sand so they can be lifted out to create planting pockets.

3. If you don't have a view, you can protect the terrace with a hedge or informal planting of trees and shrubs. This is an excellent wind screen for open terraces because the leaves and twigs sponge up the wind to such an extent that there is little air movement on the lee side. And it is also an excellent screen for a roofed terrace if you want some air movement but not too much.

For all-season protection, plant dense needled evergreens which can be held to manageable size by pruning or shearing. The list includes arborvitae, sawara false cypress, hemlock, English yew,

To protect terrace from winds driving off the Pacific Ocean while retaining a view of the ocean, a high wall of plate glass was built around the windward sides.

Hicks yew and yew pine. Broadleaf evergreens such as mountain laurel and boxwood can also be used, but their larger leaves don't control wind quite as effectively as slender needles.

If protection is required only in warm weather, deciduous plants are just as good as broadleaf evergreens. Among the best—because you can prune or shear them—are glossy abelia, Japanese barberry, spreading cotoneaster, winged euonymus, privet, flowering quince, Russian olive, cutleaf stephanandra and tallhedge.

Once a terrace is roofed and screened, an imaginative homeowner can have a field day dreaming up ways to heat it.

If you love a log fire, the two simplest ways to satisfy the urge are to build a fire pit and put in a Franklin stove. A fire pit is nothing more than a round or square depression—a saucer, if you like—in the terrace floor or raised a foot or so above the floor.

Despite its roof and thick privet hedge, this Nantucket porch was so buffeted by the prevailing wind that the owners recently put in a wall of windows to stop the blast without losing light.

Make a large hole in the roof directly overhead. On a still night, most of the smoke will escape as it should, and you can console yourself with the thought that whatever strays from the designated path helps to drive away bugs. A good way to double the warmth you receive from the fire is to cover the ceiling around the hole with reflecting aluminum foil or flashing metal.

Franklin stoves and modern equivalents such as the acorn fireplace are less romantic than a fire pit but more effective because as the metal heats up it radiates warmth in all directions. The two rules about installing a stove are: (1) It must be set out 3 ft. from a combustible wall and (2) it must stand on a noncombustible surface which extends 1 ft. beyond the hearth and 6 in. beyond the other three sides. If your building code permits, the flue through the roof can be made of a few sections of ordinary stove pipe. But a much safer chimney is a prefabricated, insulated unit like that used for many indoor fireplaces and heating plants. In either case, the top of the chimney should be a minimum of 3 ft. above a flat roof; 2 ft. above the ridge of a pitched roof.

You can build a much handsomer fireplace of brick, stone or concrete block and use it also for barbecuing. See chapter 15.

Gas heaters of several types are available. The most elaborate is a steel fireplace which is open on four sides and has a raised hearth with gas logs in the center. A pyramid-shaped hood above the fire funnels the fumes into an insulated flue which runs through the roof.

Most gas heaters, however are shaped like tall ornamental lampposts. Those that have vertical burners and give off heat only to one side are placed around the edges of a terrace. Others which radiate heat downward from an umbrellalike hood are placed in the center of the terrace. (The same type of heater is available without a post for hanging from a roof.) Most of the heaters burn natural gas and must be permanently installed. Those burning LP gas are portable.

A final way to heat a terrace is to embed electric heating cables in a concrete masonry floor. Thus the floor becomes a giant radiator which directs heat rays at people, objects and surfaces in the area above and which also adds to your comfort by warming your feet. Efficiency is quite high, especially on a terrace that is roofed and partially enclosed by walls; but the system is slower to produce comfortable conditions than other systems because the floor takes time to warm up. On the other hand, the terrace stays warm for a long time after the heater is turned off.

Radiant floor installations are made either with individual cables arranged in a gridlike pattern or with prefabricated mats in which the cables are sandwiched between wire or fiber mesh. The latter are preferable mainly because installation is easier and there's less chance for errors in layout. Whichever is used, the cables are placed 2 in. below the surface of exposed-aggregate concrete paving or on top of the slab which serves as the base for bricks, flagstones, slates and tiles.

Cooling a Terrace   This is harder than heating a terrace, because while you can take positive steps to raise terrace temperature, no practical refrigeration method exists for lowering temperature. Nevertheless, there are things you can do to make a terrace feel cooler on blistering days.

Shade, obviously, is essential; and nothing equals a big tree as a shade maker. It actually lowers the temperature in the immediate vicinity as the leaves transpire. Furthermore, it looks cool; and when a breeze rustles the leaves, it makes you "think" cool.

But unfortunately, big trees don't develop overnight; so you may have to build a roof. The arid west favors the open sun roof because it lets in some sun as well as giving shade and also permits a constant circulation of air through the terrace. In other areas, a solid roof usually is preferred because it gives shelter from the rain. To cool a terrace effectively, however, the roof must be built to satisfy two points. First, it must be opaque to give complete shade. Roofs of translucent fiberglass-reinforced plastic are less desirable because enough light gets through to raise the terrace temperature rather substantially. Second, if the terrace has more than one wall, open spaces should be provided between the roof and walls to let accumulated heat escape. Such a space is particularly important if there's a wall on the lee side of a terrace which is exposed to a prevailing breeze, because the breeze can then sweep right through the terrace.

Screening a terrace against the western sun is also essential. If your yard permits, plant trees at a distance from the terrace; and for maximum protection, use species which are covered with foliage from the top all the way down to the ground. Norway spruces and willows are good examples, but there are many others.

Evergreens are the best for warm climates, where the terrace is used the year round; but in cold climates, deciduous species are the top choice because when they lose their leaves the sun gets through to warm the terrace and make it livable on cool autumn days.

If you don't have space for trees or if you have a western view you cannot give up, the sun screen must be erected close to the terrace. Vines or climbing roses growing on a trellis are particularly desirable because, like trees, they look cool, make cooling sounds and give off moisture. If you have a view, however, a man-made screen which can be adjusted to let you enjoy the view is a better choice. Roll-down shades of canvas, woven reeds or wood strips are most often used. A more elaborate alternative, if you have a roofed terrace, is to install large panels of pierced plywood or hardboard which can be pulled open and shut like a wall of sliding doors.

Keeping the air stirred up increases comfort even though it doesn't really affect the temperature of the terrace; and you can do it easily and cheaply with any portable electric fan. Or you might take a leaf out of the book of the many southerners who have installed big, slow-turning ceiling fans like those once widely used in stores.

Further to enhance the cooling effect of a fan or of a natural breeze, put in plants near the terrace which will rustle in the breeze. All plants do this, of course, but some are more responsive and make prettier sounds than others. These include bamboo and heavenly bamboo, European birches, honey locusts, jacarandas, Russian olives, weeping willows and white pines.

Water is your best friend on a hot terrace, however. It not only gives an illusion of coolness but in dry climates it can also be used actually to lower the temperature.

The mere sight of water makes you feel cool even when you're not. This is one reason why you might build a little pool on your terrace or within sight of it. But the sound of water is even better—especially when you can see it.

Building a little fountain or waterfall is fun. And easy.

To construct the pool required for either one, use bricks and/or concrete. For a pool with perpendicular walls, pour a 4-in.-thick concrete bottom on a 4 to 6-in. base of gravel. Mix the concrete in the proportions of 1 sack Portland cement, 2¼ cu. ft. sand

(Top, left) *Raised pool in the middle of a complex of terraces. The area around the pool is used mainly for perching and enjoying a lovely view of a valley to the left. The steps lead up to another terrace where you can relax in the shade of crab apples.* (Top, right) *Eating terrace with a rather large ornamental pool at a lower level. Low lights illuminate the water and planting.* (Center) *A simple fountain in the middle of the terrace becomes a cooling oasis in summer.* (Bottom) *Minuscule informal terrace removed from the house has a little pool into which water dribbles from the wall above.*

Set some distance from the house, this small terrace feels almost surrounded by water. Nestled below the boulders is a pool with a water spout. Behind the terrace, about 20 ft. below, is a secluded ocean bay. In this the owners have placed a gigantic water spout (just visible in the center of the picture).

and 3 cu. ft. coarse aggregate. Embed heavy steel mesh or reinforc-ing rods in the middle of the slab. When the slab hardens, build brick walls up from it. (This spares you the nuisance of building forms for poured-concrete walls.) The walls should be 8 in. thick. If they are straight, build them in two tiers, with all the bricks laid as stretchers. For curving walls, lay all the bricks in header courses. In either case, follow the directions in chapter 5 for building brick walls. If you want the walls and bottom of the pool to look alike, give them two or three coats of a cementitious coating of the type used to waterproof basements. It resembles a paint and is applied in the same way. For a closer match between walls and bottom, cover the bricks with a ½-in. layer of cement plaster made by mixing 1 part cement with 3 parts sand.

Saucer-shaped pools are easily built by digging out the ground in the shape of the pool and spreading a 4-in. thickness of fine gravel and/or sand. Shape heavy steel mesh to fit in the saucer and set it 2 in. above the gravel on small chunks of brick. Then pour in a 4-in. thickness of concrete mixed to the foregoing formula, and trowel it smooth. (Depending on the size and contours of the pool, a clean garden trowel may work better than a mason's trowel. Use the palms of your hands, too.)

Put a drain in the pool only if there is some place to drain the water to. In that case, install a vertical 6-in.-long pipe at the lowest point in the bottom and connect it with an elbow to a plastic pipe which carries the water away. Use pipes about 1½ in. in diameter. To close the drain opening, use a swimming pool winterizing plug.

If you forgo a drain, you can bail out a small pool with a bucket or use a portable submersible pump in a large pool.

To make a small water-spout type of fountain, all you need is a circulating pump. Some pumps operate submerged in the pool; others are installed at a distance and are connected to the pool by two pipes—a suction line and a return.

For a more elaborate fountain, buy a pre-engineered fountain kit. Depending on the model, kits also use pumps which are in-stalled in or out of the pool.

To create a waterfall, you need some sort of spout or ledge from which the water drops into a pool or basin. A pump takes the water from the pool and raises it to the top of the falls. That's all there is to it.

A rustic New England terrace behind an ancient, but not-so-rustic house. The rectangular box in the foreground is a silent glistening pool which the owner uses as a miniature plunge.

Whether you build a waterfall or a fountain, two points must be noted:

1. The size of the pump or fountain kit depends on the size and depth of the pool, how much flow you want and how high the water must be lifted. In turn, the size and depth of the pool depends on the requirements of the pump or fountain kit. It follows that all parts of the fountain or waterfall must be designed together.

2. One drawback of every garden pool is that it quickly becomes discolored and loaded with algae and dirt; and merely circulating the water through a pump and the open air does not prevent this. Hence, to keep the water clear, you must either drain and scrub the pool every few days during the summer, stock it with a carefully selected assortment of aquatic plants and animals, or chlori-

In what amounts to an alcove off the terrace to the left of the steps is an ornamental pool with an unusual fountain head that spurts water from four sides.

nate it regularly and filter the water through sand. The last is in most ways the easiest if you put in a small swimming-pool filter system instead of an ordinary circulating pump.

As air conditioners, all pools and fountains and most water-falls have psychological value only. To enjoy the real cooling effect of water, you must spray it into the air or onto a surface of the terrace.

In a hot, dry climate when water is sprayed into the air, it is evaporated by the air and the air's temperature is reduced. In any climate, when water is sprayed or otherwise applied to a surface, the surface is cooled and then draws heat from human bodies and other objects nearby. (This is the principle of radiation: the colder of two surfaces which are exposed to each other absorbs heat from the warmer surface.)

It is not difficult to take advantage of these phenomena to make your terrace more comfortable.

One thing you can do to lower temperature through evaporation is buy a humidifier which vaporizes water and sprays the fine mist across the terrace. Most humidifiers suitable for this purpose are portable or roll-around units which operate when you plug them into a 120-volt outlet. But units which are built into a wall and spray mist through a small porthole are available. Whichever design you use, it should be large enough to deliver at least 5 gal. of water per day.

Another thing you can do in a dry climate if your terrace is exposed to a prevailing breeze is to build a simple type of evaporative cooler on the windward side of the terrace. The cooler consists of a dense vine on a trellis or a heavy burlap hanging over which you drip or spray water while the wind is blowing. When the wind passes through the screen, its temperature drops.

Probably the most practical and certainly the most decorative way to cool a terrace by radiation is to build a waterfall that drops a sheet of water down over a wide, high wall. But you can obtain the same effect simply by dribbling water down a wall or spraying the wall with a hose nozzle or perforated tube.

7 Wiring and Lighting the Terrace

Even though you may find a terrace most enchanting when the only light comes from the stars and nearby house windows, there are almost certainly times when you need electricity so you can really see what you're doing, run a radio or television set or keep a pot of coffee hot for the assembled guests.

Start the electrification of your terrace by making a list of the ways you will use electricity. If the only use is for lighting, a single 15-amp, 120-volt circuit is probably all you need. But if you also occasionally need electricity for a roaster, frying pan or other small appliance, the circuit should be designed for 20-amp service. And if you plan to do a great deal of outdoor cooking, you should put in both a 15-amp, 120-volt lighting circuit and a 20-amp, 120-volt appliance circuit.

Since wiring circuits should be installed or extended only by a professional, I won't go into the details here. But you should at least understand what's involved and what materials are used.

To begin with, always specify no. 12 wire rather than no. 14 because it will carry a heavier load over a longer distance. To be sure, this may not be important at the moment; but it will permit you to extend the circuits or to increase the load at a later date.

Because it's difficult to run cables through the walls of an existing house without opening large holes for them, and because the construction of a terrace roof rarely permits cables to be concealed, all wiring which will be exposed to view should be run through neat metal raceways.

If wiring extends across a terrace, run it under the floor through large rigid conduits. Thus you can easily snake through additional wires if you ever expand the outdoor electrical installation.

Wiring that runs through planting beds in and around the terrace should also be in conduits to protect it when the beds are dug or cultivated. However, you can use direct-burial cable without conduit if your local building code permits and provided that you bury it at least 1 ft. deep and cover it with a board.

In lawn areas, direct-burial cable need be buried only 6 in. deep. Remember however, that its use may be restricted by law.

All electrical boxes, outlets and switches must be of the waterproof variety. Light fixtures must also be weatherproof.

Convenience outlets into which you plug portable lamps, cooking appliances, radios, etc., should be installed at least 18 in. above the terrace floor. In areas with heavy snow or if a terrace is exposed to drifting snow, they should be considerably higher. As a rule of thumb, you should put in one duplex outlet per 15 ft. of solid wall; but you may need more. Place them within 6 ft. of the points where you expect to use portable lamps or appliances.

Control all lights, if possible, from switches inside the house so that you can light your way onto the terrace.

If a terrace is adjacent to a swimming pool or has an ornamental pool, outlets used for appliances, tools and plug-in lamps must be installed a minimum of 10 ft. from the pool; and lighting outlets, switches and junction boxes should be at least 5 ft. from the pool. This puts them out of arm's reach of adults or children in the pool.

Also on a terrace adjacent to a swimming pool, all electrical equipment must be grounded, and all convenience outlets between 10 and 15 ft. from the pool must be protected by a ground fault circuit interrupter (also known as a GFI).

Basic Rules for Terrace Lighting

Regardless of the kind of terrace you build, there are certain hard-and-fast rules for lighting it:

1. Install enough lights of sufficient wattage so you can eat without wondering what you're putting into your mouth; play games; toss darts; illuminate the swimming pool if it's adjacent to the terrace; etc. Odds are that you won't use all or even most of the lights as often as you sit in darkness or semidarkness. But when you need them, you need them.

If there are large sliding glass doors onto the terrace, another good reason for lighting the terrace well is to allow you to see through the otherwise black, cold, mirrorlike glass when you sit indoors at night.

2. Shield all bulbs so you aren't bothered by their glare. This is standard practice indoors; and since most terrace light fixtures are similar in design to indoor fixtures, you don't have to worry much about those you mount on the ceiling and walls. But you may also install lights in the garden area immediately surrounding the terrace, and these you must watch out for.

Happily there are various ways of concealing them from direct view. You can, for instance, hide them in the foliage or branches of a tree; recess them in large cans or drain tiles sunk in the ground; or simply use fixtures with hoods and perhaps diffusers.

3. Be careful not to aim any light so it shines into your neighbors' eyes. There's always danger of angering neighbors when you mount floodlights or spotlights under the eaves, high in trees or pointing up into trees.

4. Use white light only on the terrace and in the immediate vicinity. It produces the most nearly natural effect, and brings out colors best. Yellow light makes the world look sick. Red turns green foliage brown. Green brings out the color of foliage but the green is too unnatural. Blue light is too mysterious.

Admittedly, white light attracts bugs. But if you're clever, you can foil the pests. For how to do this, see the next chapter.

**Lighting a
Roofed Terrace**

This is much like lighting a living room or family room. You can use ceiling fixtures or wall fixtures or both. And you may also use low downlights to illuminate the edges of the terrace and adjacent planting beds.

Surface-mounted ceiling fixtures with wide diffusing bowls—the type most often used indoors—are generally unsuited to terraces unless the underside of the roof is a flat, unbroken surface. But surface-mounted downlights of modern design can be attractively installed between rafters, although you need quite a few of them if you want to light the entire terrace fairly evenly. Hanging bubble lights are more efficient but take a beating from winds.

If you want to make your own ceiling fixtures, try putting rows of fluorescent tubes between the rafters and concealing them with plastic diffusing panels attached to the bottom edges of the rafters.

Covered terrace lighted by hanging bubble lights. The apple tree is floodlighted from four points to bring out the texture of the foliage and bark and to emphasize the shape of the trunks. (PHOTO BY GENERAL ELECTRIC)

Terrace roof of translucent glass is turned into a giant lighting fixture by placing two dimmer-controlled bulbs above each skylight. The plants and sculpture are accented by spotlights recessed in the roof. (**PHOTO BY JOHN WATSON, LANDSCAPE ILLUMINATOR**)

This is the same type of installation which is frequently made indoors to create a so-called luminous ceiling. For best results, the rafters should be 8 to 10 in. deep; otherwise, the tubes show up through the diffusers as distinct lines of bright light. Note that the ceiling surfaces to which the fluorescent fixtures are screwed must be covered with ¼-in.-thick asbestos-cement board as a safeguard against combustion.

If a roof is open rather than solid, overhead lighting gains glamour but loses efficiency. Instead of mounting lights below the roof or in the spaces between louvers, etc., hang them above the roof so the light coming through will be partially filtered. To direct all the light downward, use bullet fixtures and mount them on the house walls and in overhanging trees.

Wall fixtures are more commonly used on terraces because they are simple and attractive and you don't have to worry so much about whether they do or don't look right. However, if you install them only on the house wall, the outer margins of the terrace are not well lighted. But this is easily corrected by mounting additional lights on the posts supporting the roof or by mounting lights with diffusers under the roof overhangs.

Lighting an Open Terrace

It's harder to get a high level of illumination on an open terrace than on a roofed terrace, but the lighting can be much more glamorous. My favorite way of going at the job is to install one or more bullet fixtures with floodlamps high up in a tree and aim the light downward through the branches. (No diffusing lenses are needed on the fixtures if they are properly concealed.)

Another approach which produces a lower light level is to aim a floodlamp up into a low-hanging deciduous tree from a concealed fixture in the ground. The leaves act as reflectors.

Still another way to produce a low light level is to direct a floodlamp up and down or across a white-painted wall. (But never aim it straight at the wall.) The effect is particularly delightful if shrubs with interesting branches and delicate foliage are planted out from the wall so they are silhouetted against it.

If you are content with a very low light level—one that lets you gaze at the stars but still lets you see where you're going—you might install low downlights around the sides of the terrace.

A final possibility on a terrace surrounded by an openwork fence or translucent plastic fence is to place floodlights outside and let the light filter through.

Floodlights aimed down from the trees light the terrace. Specially made lighted stars add a note of excitement. (PHOTO BY JOHN WATSON)

Small, open terrace is lighted by three low mushroom fixtures and a floodlamp angled at the fence from the eaves of the house. (PHOTO BY GENERAL ELECTRIC)

**Lighting a
Barbecue Area**

This is the one place on the terrace where you must have plenty of light so you can tell whether the steak has reached just the right point of juicy doneness.

Use two 75-watt floodlamps in reflectors mounted to either side of and above the grill.

**Lighting the
Garden Beyond the
Terrace**

Your garden can be an entrancing backdrop for your terrace at night as well as during the day. There are many ways to make it this way with light; but since this isn't a garden-lighting book per se, I won't attempt to cover all.

Generally, the terrace is the most brightly lighted part of the entire garden area. The middle ground just beyond is the dimmest. The background is of medium intensity.

Unless you have some unusually interesting plants or other features in the middle ground, don't bother to light the area.

The simplest and one of the prettiest ways to light the background is to illuminate a single tree. If the tree has open foliage and particularly if it has a high canopy (like an elm or old sugar

Lighting the terrace and garden beyond turns the picture window from a black, impenetrable mirror into a transparent glass pane. You get the same result when you light the garden beyond a screened terrace. (PHOTO BY WESTINGHOUSE)

maple), place a floodlamp at ground level or in the lower part of the tree and aim it upward.

If the tree has a handsome trunk (for instance, a white birch or cork tree) or branch structure (an oak or crape myrtle), install a pair of lights at ground level—one on the right side of the tree; the other on the left—and aim them into the tree. To avoid a flat look, use a stronger light on one side than the other; or use a flood-lamp in one fixture and a spot in the other.

Lighting so You Can See Beyond a Screened Porch

If you sit on a lighted screened porch at night, the screenwire becomes a barrier between the porch and the world beyond, and you feel vaguely uncomfortable, hemmed in. To prevent this, it is necessary to light the yard or garden.

An easy but not very attractive way to do this is to light the garden just beyond the screens with 150-watt floodlamps mounted on the terrace roof at least 2 ft. above the tops of the screens. Aim them outward at a 45° angle.

A better solution is to use floodlamps and spots to light specific trees, shrubs, walls or ornaments in the garden.

Lights recessed in the roof overhang just above the sliding glass doors are designed to illuminate the deck and also to make it possible to see the deck when sitting inside.

Falling water brings a feeling of coolness to the terrace; light makes the waterfalls beautiful—a focal point on the terrace.
(PHOTO BY JOHN WATSON)

Low-voltage Lighting

Twelve-volt lighting is often highly touted as the best way to light a garden. Reasons: It doesn't give a dangerous shock. It's easy to install because all you have to do is plug a transformer into a convenience outlet and run wires and lights from there anywhere you like. And it gives a softer light than you get with high-wattage 120-volt lamps.

In spite of all this, I remain a believer in the old-fashioned 120-volt system because it is more versatile and more permanent and has a lower line loss of current.

But the main trouble with the 12-volt system for terrace lighting is that you can use it only to run lights; it's no good for appliances and other electrical equipment. In addition, while it may be easier to install 12-volt cables in the garden (though I question this except in communities which ban the use of direct-burial 120-volt cable), you have exactly the same problems you have with 120-volt cables when you try to run them through the walls and roof of a terrace.

Enchanting scene is achieved by bathing the wall, flowers and tree trunks in white light from floodlights high in the branches. The Chinese lantern emits a reddish light simulating a flickering flame. The terrace is paved with large rounds of concrete set in gravel. (PHOTO BY JOHN WATSON)

Gas Lighting   Most gas lights are post lights with a burner enclosed in glass under a metal hood. But there are lights which can be hung from a ceiling or mounted on walls; and there are also Hawaiian torches spouting large flames which cannot be extinguished by rain or wind.

All gas lights get their fuel through a small underground copper tube. Installation of lights and tubes must be made professionally. Once they are turned on, most post lights operate day and night and use about as much gas as a kitchen range. However, there are ways to turn them on and off and control the intensity of the light.

Lighting the Terrace   See chapter 16.
for a Party

⑧ Beating the Bugs

Bugs are not an inevitability on a terrace. Some months ago I was commiserating with the people who own the terrace shown on page 22, because it is totally surrounded by a vast marsh. "Bugs must drive you crazy," I said. "Not at all," Phil retorted. "We rarely have a one. You see, this is a tidal marsh and the water moving in and out never gives insects a chance to propagate."

It would be nice if more terraces had tidal marshes nearby. But they don't. So for many people bugs are a problem—sometimes a miserable problem.

Lighting the Terrace Without Attracting Bugs

If you live in an area where insects are troublesome only at night, there's no reason why you have to retire indoors when the sun goes down. You can enjoy your terrace as much as ever—even if it is brightly lighted with white light.

Impossible, you say? Bugs love white light. Only yellow light keeps them away.

No, yellow light has no such magic power. It neither repels bugs nor kills them. Its only virtue is that it is less attractive than white light; therefore it doesn't draw so many bugs. But this is a dubious advantage when you consider how ghastly people, plants and other objects look in yellow light.

The easy way to make your terrace attractive and usable with white light and yet keep it free of phototropic insects is to install about 40 ft. from the terrace an ordinary blue light or "black" (ultraviolet) light. The insects can't resist either, but especially a black light.

When buying a black light (you need only one for the average-size property), be sure to get the kind that is made of dark red-purple glass. Others require filters. Use the bulb in a fixture which protects it from rain and snow; mount the fixture in a tree or on a building about 8 to 10 ft. above ground, and aim it toward the terrace.

One weakness of black lights and blue lights is that they don't kill insects. So if you have murderous tendencies, you may prefer to go one step further and put in an insect trap. These cost a great deal more than a simple light bulb and fixture; but when insects drawn to them by the built-in black lights pass through the covering grid, they're electrocuted. In some models the bugs drop through to the ground where the birds can devour them; in others, the bugs end up in bags or containers which must be emptied.

Screening a Terrace
Over the years it seems to me there has been a trend away from screened porches, terraces or what-have-you; and I suppose there are two reasons: modern insecticides are more effective than those of yesteryear; and people today are happier if there is nothing— not even a piece of mesh—separating them from the great outdoors.

Yet for many people screened terraces are a must because they provide the only positive escape from bugs at all hours of the day and night.

To some people screens are also desirable because they reduce sunlight on a terrace approximately 25 per cent.

If you come to the conclusion that you must screen your terrace, the first thing you have to decide is whether to build the screens yourself. At first glance, it appears to be a lot of work with a certain amount of difficulty. But in reality, while it's not a job anyone will complete overnight, it should be relatively easy for you if you have any facility with tools. Certainly it will save a lot of money.

The second point to decide is which kind of screen wire (also called screencloth and screening) you will use. Four conventional types plus a specialty product are on the market. In choosing between the conventional types you should consider the width, mesh, color and material.

WIDTHS Standard width for all metal screening ranges from 2 to 4 ft. Fiberglass ranges from 2 to 7 ft.

MESH For maximum protection, use an 18 x 16 mesh. This means there are 18 squares per inch in one direction, 16 in the other direction. For slightly better visibility and less shade, use 18 x 14 mesh.

COLOR Galvanized-steel and bronze screening come in only one color. The former is light; the other, dark (after weathering). Aluminum and fiberglass screening come in various colors. In all cases, darker colors give better visibility; light colors reflect more heat rays and keep the terrace cooler.

MATERIAL Galvanized steel is inexpensive but short-lived because it rusts out rapidly.

Bronze is the most durable screening but costs a fortune.

Aluminum is durable and fire-resistant. It doesn't rust but in coastal areas and industrial atmospheres it corrodes and acquires an unsightly, uneven oxide. On the other hand, it has the strength to spring back into shape when hit or pushed head on; but when struck a glancing blow with a rather sharp instrument, such as a dog's claw, it may develop a shallow crease which can't be ironed out.

Fiberglass screening, on the other hand, doesn't show creases; but while it has pretty good resistance to impact, it tends to belly when a child or anyone else leans against it or strikes it, and you have to loosen and renail it to make it flat again. It is rustproof, corrosionproof and fireproof (though it will melt if you touch it with something very hot).

The specialty screen wire is made of aluminum and has vertical rows of wires and horizontal rows of tiny slanted louvers. It's designed to give maximum shade and insect protection without seriously reducing air circulation. You can see out from inside (though not as well as with conventional screening); but your neighbors can't see in.

Building Screens for a Roofed Terrace

Terrace screens are built in large sections to fit between the posts supporting the roof and between the floor and roof beams or rafters. Generally they are constructed so they can be taken down and stored (although most people don't actually do this); but if you want to build them in permanently, there is no rule saying you can't. In either case, one of your main aims should be to construct the screens so they don't obstruct the view any more than necessary.

For framing lumber use redwood, cypress or any other knot-free softwood which is thoroughly saturated with wood preservative. For take-down screens use 1½ x 3-in. boards; however, it may be wise—especially if you have children—to make the bottom rail of 1½ x 6-in. lumber in order to get the screen wire above easy kicking range. For permanent screens, use 2 x 3 or 2 x 4-in. timbers.

Buy the screen door that opens out to the garden. Because it moves, it takes a beating, and must therefore be put together by experienced craftsmen with special tools.

To build permanent screens, cut the framing lumber to fit horizontally between the roof posts or between the sides of the house and the roof posts. Nail one piece to the beam or rafter. Fasten another piece to the floor directly underneath. If the floor

This wing incorporating a raised screened porch was recently added to the old Victorian house. It was necessitated by the fact that the area sometimes swarms with mosquitoes, which make it almost impossible to use the ground-level open terrace behind the porch (and wellhouse).

is masonry, drive screws into lead anchors set in the floor. Use nails if the floor is wood.

Cut lumber to fit between the top and bottom rails, and nail pieces to the posts and/or house wall to complete a large frame. These vertical members are called stiles.

Cut more pieces of lumber to fit between the top and bottom rails and use them to divide the large frame into vertical sections of equal width. The width of the sections depends on the overall width of the large frame and the width of screen wire that you use. The section containing the screen door should be just a fraction wider than the door. The odds are that the widths of the section across the front of the terrace will be different from those across the sides; and if you install the door in one side, the fixed screen sections in that side will not be the same width as the sections in the other side. Whatever the layout, try not to make any section less than 4 ft. wide. Fasten the intermediate stiles to the rails by toenailing with 5-in. galvanized nails; and countersink the nail heads so they can be concealed later with putty or spackle.

Install a horizontal middle rail in each section of the screen frame and toenail it to the stiles. Since one of the purposes of this rail is to protect the screen wire from furniture which may be pushed back against it, place the rail at the same height as the backs of your terrace chairs. But before freezing on this position, make sure that when you sit in the chairs the rail does not block your view of the garden.

Apply a priming coat of paint or first coat of stain when the frames are finished.

Fasten the screen wire to the outside surfaces of the frame with ¼ or ⅜ in. tacks. The edges of the wire should lap over the framing members about ¾ in. Use galvanized tacks for galvanized screening: copper tacks for bronze screening; aluminum tacks for aluminum screening; aluminum or copper tacks for fiberglass screening.

Tack the screen wire to the top rail first. Tack one corner; pull the wire taut without stretching it out of shape; tack the other corner; and then put a tack in the middle. Then fill in with tacks spaced about 2 in. apart.

Pull the screen wire down tight to the floor and tack it to the bottom rail. This is a difficult maneuver because there isn't much

This spectacular two-story deck is equipped with enormous screens which can be rolled down across the openings like window shades. The screens had to be made out of fiberglass by a sailmaker. As the picture suggests, there is an upper balcony at the back of the main deck.

space to work and because you must hold the wire, set a tack and hammer it in all at once. Get someone to help you.

Then finish tacking the screen wire to the stiles and the middle rail, and cut off the excess wire with an old knife.

Cover the edges of the screen wire with ½-in. screen moldings or half rounds which you have primed with paint or stained. On intermediate stiles to which you have tacked two pieces of screen wire, use one molding to cover both edges. Also put moldings over the tacks in the middle rails. Miter the moldings at corners. Use 1-in. or smaller galvanized steel brads to nail the moldings. Countersink the heads.

Since the door to the garden probably isn't as tall as the screens, a middle rail must be installed over it and screen wire stretched between this and the top rail. Swing the door in or out. When closed, it should bear against stops nailed to the sides of the timbers framing the door. Stops are thin wood moldings available in various sizes from a lumber yard.

Building screens you can take down is more difficult.

Measure the spaces between roof posts or between posts and the house wall very carefully at the floor line and also at the roof line. Plumb the posts and wall with a carpenter's level or plumb line. You may find that, because something is out of plumb, a few of the screens have to be trimmed along an edge if they are to fit tight, without gaps. To simplify later handling, it is best not to make the screens more than 4 ft. wide; but don't make them any smaller than this than you have to. All the screens in any one wall should be the same width; but in the door wall, the door will probably be narrower than the screens.

Join the rails and stiles at the corners of the screen frames with half-lap joints. In these, identical notches to half the depth of the wood are made in the pieces being joined. Cut the notches with a fine-toothed saw. Sand the surfaces smooth. Then apply resorcinol glue to one side of the joint, and stick the pieces together. Secure them with a couple of 1¼-in. aluminum or brass flathead screws.

The middle rail is joined to the stiles by one-third-two-thirds lap joints. The length of the rail should equal the total width of the screen frame. In the ends, cut notches 3 in. long (equal to the width of the lumber used) and to two thirds of the depth of the rail. On the *terrace-side* surfaces of the stiles, cut notches to receive the ends of the rails (in other words, they are 3 in. high and to one third of the depth of the lumber). Then sand, glue, fit and screw the rail to the stiles. (This kind of lap joint is used instead of a half lap because it does not weaken the stiles to the same extent.)

Prime or stain the completed frames. Then tack screen wire to the outside faces of each frame; apply the moldings; and cut off the excess screen wire. If you have difficulty stretching metal screen wire tight by hand (fiberglass is easy), here is a way to simplify operations:

Lay a couple of short 2 x 4s on the floor about 7 ft. apart. Lay two long 2 x 4s over these at right angles. The space between them should be about 6 in. less than the width of the frame to which you are applying screening. On top of these and at right angles to them lay two short lengths of 1-in. boards. Space them apart by the length of the screen. Place the screen frame on this rack. Slip a C clamp over each stile and the long 2 x 4 underneath, and tighten the clamps until the stiles are bowed downward about ½ in. Then tack the screen wire to the top and bottom rails. When the clamps are removed, the stiles will straighten and pull the wire tight. Then tack the wire to the stiles.

Hold the screens in place on the terrace with wood stops similar to those used around door frames. Nail the stops to the bottom of the roof beam or rafter and to the sides of the roof posts and house wall. Fasten the bottom stop to the floor with nails or with screws driven into lead anchors (depending on what the floor is made of).

Set the screens upright against the inside edges of the stops and, while someone holds them, install hooks and eyes around the outside edges. Drive the hooks into the screens; the eyes into the stops.

If adjacent screens fit tightly, there is no need to seal the joints between them. If a joint is wide, however, center a 1-in.-wide strip of thin wood over it and nail the strip to one of the screen frames.

The screen door should always be hung next to a post or house wall to which it can be hinged. Install a short screen over it. Fasten this to the post or wall with an angle iron, and to the adjacent full-length screen frame with a straight mending plate. Nail strips of ½-in.-thick wood to the bottom of the short screen and the side of the adjacent full-length screen to serve as stops against which the door closes.

119

One knotty little problem you may encounter in building either permanent or take-down screens is how to seal the joint between a screen and a house wall that is built of shingles, clapboards or rough stones. The solution is to scribe the stile abutting the wall to the wall. The alternative is to insert a narrow board between the stile and the wall and to scribe and then nail it to the wall.

Whichever method you use, cut the board to be scribed to the height of the screen frame. Place it against the wall and make certain it is plumb. In order to make and hold it plumb, you may have to insert small wedges. Then open a pair of dividers or a compass a fraction wider than the widest gap between the board and wall. Starting at the top, hold one leg of the dividers against the wall and the other on the board, and slowly draw the dividers down the wall all the way to the bottom. This will leave a scratch or pencil line on the board which exactly parallels the contours of the wall. Trim the board to this line.

Building Screens for an Open Terrace

When you screen an open terrace, you must screen the roof as well as the sides. Because of difficulties in constructing the roof screens, the installation should be permanent; consequently it should be made only in areas with very little or no snow. In heavy snow country a screened roof will sag badly and perhaps be ruined.

Screen enclosures for open terraces are sometimes built with metal frames; but leave this to experts. You should use 2 x 4s of redwood, cypress or preservative-treated wood.

Lay out the framework for each wall—one at a time—on the terrace floor. (This is the way walls for houses are built today.) The bottom horizontal member of each wall is the soleplate. The top horizontal member is the top plate and should consist of two 2 x 4s nailed together flat side to flat side. The vertical members nailed between the plates correspond to studs. The spaces between the studs in each wall should be equal, and ideally they should be at least 46½ in. wide. Nail 2 x 4s between the studs to serve as the middle rails.

When a wall is completed, tilt it upward and brace it. When all the walls are upright, plumb them carefully and make certain they are at right angles to one another. Then nail them together. Spike the innermost stud in each end wall to the wall of the house. Anchor the soleplates to the terrace floor with lead anchors or with spikes.

For simplicity, make the roof flat. Nail a 2 x 4-in. ledger strip to the house wall at the same height as the top plates. For rafters use 2 x 4s and lay them between the ledger strip and the top plate at the front of the terrace (or lay them from one end of the terrace to the other if this is a shorter distance). Space the rafters equally and no more than 4 ft. center to center. Attach them to the sides of the ledger strip and top plate with metal hangers.

The screen wire is laid parallel to the rafters and tacked along the edges to them. But no matter how tight you pull the wire, it is likely to sag unless you provide cross supports. The easiest way to make these is to staple 18-gauge aluminum wire across the tops of the rafters at 2- to 4-ft. intervals. But a better solution—because it's a little more attractive and helps to strengthen the entire enclosure—is to nail 2 x 4s between the rafters, perpendicular to them. The spaces between the cross blocks should be equal, but no more than 4 ft. wide.

Tack the roof screening to the tops of the rafters, cross blocks, top plates and ledger strip. Tack the wall screening to the outside edges of the soleplates, studs, top plates and middle rails. Cover the edges with moldings.

Because a screen enclosure of this type is very airy and uncluttered, the outside door will look best if it is the same height as the walls. To ensure the strongest possible joints, let a millwork shop make the door frame for you out of 2 x 4 lumber.

⑨ Enclosing the Terrace

One of our local builders maintains that he's particularly pleased to land terrace-building jobs because they add up to five years of remunerative work.

How come?

"Well," he says, "the first year I build the terrace. The second year you ask me to roof it. The third year you ask me to screen it. The fourth year you ask me to close it in. And the fifth year you ask me to build another terrace."

It could be he's right.

Anyway, it's a certainty that many terraces or porches, etc., are eventually enclosed. Usually this just happens. But sometimes it's a long-range plan. Right now one of our friends is starting to build a terrace which she ultimately intends to close in to make what is often called a sun porch or Florida room.

Planning a Terrace for Future Enclosure

At the time you build a terrace, if you have even the faintest idea that you will someday enclose it, you should construct it accordingly. True, it will add to the initial cost; but it should save a pile of money in the long run. And you will also wind up with a better room.

Here are the steps to take:

Locate the terrace so that, when enclosed, it will not make the room off which it opens too dark and also so that you can enter it without walking through a room. This isn't a must rule if you are simply going to glass in the terrace—which is usually what happens. But it is a rule if you turn the terrace into an honest-to-goodness room with solid exterior walls pierced with normal-size windows, because that will cut off much of the daylight to the inner room. That you won't like.

The business about walking through one room to get to another room doesn't bother many people. But it's a rule that good architects always follow because, if they don't, the first room turns into a corridor, the privacy of its occupants is destroyed and its furnishings are worn out. That's why they put in halls. And that, in effect, is what you should do when you build your terrace: make it reachable through a hall as well as, say, the living room or kitchen.

Raise the terrace off the ground. If it has a masonry floor, it needs to be raised only about 6 in. so that water can't work its way into the room and the walls will be protected against decay and termites. If the floor is wood, however, you must provide a minimum of 18 in. between the ground and the bottoms of the floor joists so that workmen can get underneath to install heating pipes or ducts and to insulate the floor.

Construct the terrace floor so it will be completely resistant to frost action. If you build a wood porch or deck, be sure that the concrete piers supporting it extend from below the frost line to 6 in. above ground level. If the floor is cf concrete masonry, a simple "floating" slab comparable to the types described in chapter 4 should be built only if the soil is so well drained that frost presents no problems. In other words, it must be almost pure sand or gravel. Around the perimeter of the terrace, the slab is 1 ft. deep; the large middle area, 4 in. The entire slab is poured on a 4-in.-deep base of crushed rock which is covered with a vapor barrier of heavy polyethylene film.

On soil that is subject to frost action, surround the terrace with foundation walls extending below the frost line and rest the terrace floor on these. Within the foundations, directly under the floor, is a 4-in. base of crushed stone covered with polyethylene film. A 1-to-3-in.-thick rigid, waterproof insulating board is inserted between the edges of the slab and the foundations and extends about 2 ft. under the slab.

Make provision for heating the enclosed terrace. If your heating plant has sufficient capacity, you can use it to heat the terrace room if you install the necessary ducts or pipes in a masonry floor at the

This terrace was planned at the outset for indoor and outdoor use. The outdoor area is on two levels. The indoor area, with large sliding glass doors, is on the same level as the upper area outdoors. The entire terrace is oriented to a view of Lake Erie.

Big panes of insulated glass keep this enclosed Minnesota terrace comfortable in the winter. Some of the panes are fixed; others are hinged at the top to open outward.
(PHOTO BY ANDERSON CORP.)

time you construct it. Although these should be completely covered, you can crack through the surface of the floor to get at them when the time comes.

Enclosing an Existing Terrace

I assume that what you want is a glass-walled sun room. But don't try building it yourself. The job is too difficult. You also run some risk that, unless you constructed the floor in the way described, it may be heaved and cracked by frost and the walls may be similarly affected. (But a professional builder cannot prevent such problems either.)

Jalousies are probably the number one choice of most people who enclose roofed terraces. They are aluminum-framed windows with numerous narrow, horizontal, unframed panes which are opened outward with a crank. You can slant the louvers downward to admit air but not rain, or turn them straight out or even upward. Thus they are ideal for controlling air movement through the terrace in the summer; and yet they can be closed tight enough in winter to prevent entrance of moisture. But despite claims, they cannot be closed tight enough to prevent air leakage; consequently you should use them only if you live in a warm climate or if you substitute storm sash for the screens with which the windows are equipped.

Jalousies are built in a great range of sizes; but to use them on a terrace, you must raise them off the floor at least a few inches on a wall. This takes away a little of the feeling of being outdoors. The other drawback of the windows is that while you can see out of them, you can't walk out through them.

If you put in large plate-glass windows, you run into the same

124

problems. And you cannot open the room up so completely, although this doesn't mean you cannot have ample ventilation by hinging some of the windows as in the photograph on page 124.

On the other hand, the unbroken panes permit a much clearer view of the garden than is possible with jalousies. There is no air or moisture leakage whatever; and if you install double-paned insulating glass, heat loss from the room is reduced substantially.

*Florida terrace in a breezeway between house and garage is enclosed with jalousies. An orange tree, an outstanding ornamental, grows in front. (*PHOTO BY AGRICULTURAL EXTENSION SERVICE*)*

To me, however, the most exciting way of enclosing a roofed terrace is to wall it around with sliding glass doors that extend from floor to ceiling. Thus, simply by pushing the doors to the side, you can walk in and out through all the walls. And when you are relaxing inside, you feel one with the world around you. The view out is unobstructed. Heat loss is held to a minimum if the doors have insulating glass. In comparison with jalousies, the only thing you lose is unrestricted ventilation.

Enclosing an Unroofed Terrace

Of course, you can build a roof and then wall the terrace in with jalousies, plate glass or sliding glass doors. But there is a much easier solution: buy a lean-to greenhouse or glass swimming-pool enclosure. There are numerous styles and sizes to choose from; but

125

pool enclosures which have large sliding glass doors in the walls are particularly suitable because you can open them up in summer to a greater extent than the ordinary greenhouse.

Enclosing a Wood Deck or Porch

Enclose these as you would a masonry terrace. If the deck has cracks between the floor boards, lay a new floor of boards or parquet blocks on top.

Heating the New Room

The first step is to insulate the floor as much as possible. If it's a masonry slab, dig down around the edges and cover them with rigid, waterproof insulating boards. Use 1-in.-thick boards in warm climates; 2-in. in intermediate climates; 3-in. in cold climates. The boards should cover the edges of the slab from the top to the bottom. Hold them in place with asphalt roofing cement.

If you have a raised deck or porch, install 6-in.-thick fiberglass or mineral-wool insulating batts between the floor joists. The batts should have a vapor barrier on the upper side. To hold the batts in place, nail chicken wire to the bottoms of the joists.

If the roof of the terrace is similar to your house roof, insulate it with 6-in. batts with a vapor barrier on the underside. Staple the batts between the rafters, and build a ceiling of gypsum board, wood or plywood underneath.

Heat can be supplied in a number of ways.

If your furnace or boiler has reserve capacity, extend ducts or pipes to the terrace and install registers or radiators. Ideally these should be located next to the glass walls so they will counteract the cold air coming through; but if this can be done only by breaking open the floor, place them against the house wall.

If your heating plant isn't large enough to heat the terrace room, your best bet is to install electric or gas heating. Electric baseboards are ideal if the glass walls of the room do not extend all the way down to the floor. Otherwise, install heating coils in the ceiling or build wall heaters into the house wall. Small gas heaters which resemble room air conditioners can be built into the outer walls of a terrace room. The alternative on a very large terrace is to recess a wall furnace into the house wall.

10 Swimming-pool Terraces

Putting an in-ground swimming pool in the middle of or immediately adjacent to a terrace is more and more the thing to do. There are five reasons:

1. The pool becomes the focus of family life. It pulls young and old together.

2. The pool is easy to supervise even when the parents are going about their work indoors.

3. The house becomes the bathhouse: there's no need for separate dressing rooms or toilet facilities.

4. Swimmers can get quickly to the front door or telephone when the bell rings.

5. If the terrace has to be raised, the cost of excavating for the pool is reduced.

But there are also reasons why a swimming pool on the terrace is a poor idea:

1. It completely dominates family life: you just can't get away from it.

2. The glare from the water is reflected into the house, where it fades fabrics, furniture, floors, etc.

3. For the onlooker, life on the terrace is a nightmare of puddled pavement, wet bodies, splashing, scrambling children, noise and the sometimes not-so-subtle smell of chlorine.

4. During summer parties there is the ever-present risk of guests falling into the pool.

5. In winter, unless you live in a warm climate where the pool is kept in operation, you are afflicted by the sight of the pool covered with faded vinyl or filled with leaves and algae.

You can see that I am not partial to swimming pools in or near terraces near the house. It's far better to move the pool well away from the house and give it its own terrace (which is commonly known as a pool deck). But I'm afraid my voice is lost.

But do, at least, plan your pool with the terrace in mind and vice versa.

Although it causes problems, the rim of the pool should be slightly higher than the terrace so that when rain falls or you hose down the terrace, the water will not run into the pool with a load of dirt. The most practical way to accomplish this is to surround the

Vast walled terrace incorporating an intricately shaped swimming pool opens out from the house (behind camera). This is how it looks at night. (PHOTO BY JOHN WATSON)

pool with a bull-nose coping which is about 1 in. higher at the very edge of the pool than along the back side. An alternative is to slant the paving away from the pool for 2 or 3 ft. on all sides, and make a barely perceptible trough to collect the water and funnel it into floor drains.

The entire terrace should be covered with paving which is non-glary and cool and comfortable for swimmers. Pink bricks and gray flagstones are good. Kool Deck is especially good because it is cooler than most pavings, but its light pastel colors may seem rather glary.

The terrace must have ample space so just-sitters won't be overwhelmed by swimmers. Ideally, the sitting area should be at a somewhat higher level than the pool to emphasize the distinction between the two areas and keep swimmers where they belong. This also makes it simpler to keep water from draining into the pool.

Because wet bodies dislike cool breezes, a pool terrace is more likely to require a wind screen than a nonpool terrace. If you use plants for the screen, provide a space of no less than 4 ft. between the ends of the branches and the pool. This keeps swimmers from being scratched. More important, it helps to prevent leaves, twigs, etc., from drifting into the pool.

In most communities, the entire terrace and pool area must by law be completely surrounded by a fence at least 4 ft. high with gates which can be locked against children. Since this adds nothing to the beauty of the area, the best practice is to fence the entire back yard.

Although this swimming pool is very close to the house, it is set far enough below it so that swimmers don't have to get in the hair of nonswimmers relaxing on the two-level terrace.

A vast swimming-pool terrace in Phoenix. Everything—even the rooms in the house—is on the same level. The exceptionally deep roof overhang gives ample protection against the sun, but the glare from the paving (Kool Deck) is considerable. (PHOTO BY ARIZONA PHOTOGRAPHIC ASSOCIATES)

If the pool has an underwater light, put it into the side or end aiming away from the house. A dimmer switch is often used to reduce brightness when the terrace is occupied.

Install the pool pump and filter where the noise they make will not be heard. Putting them into a pit is recommended because they are protected against freezing and the pipe runs are short. In

(Left) The terrace first pictured in this book as seen from the deck at the end of the swimming pool (right). Although pool and terrace are within view and earshot of each other, they are separated by a rocky gully which can be crossed easily only on a wide wooden gangplank.

addition, the pump does not have to work as hard as it does when above the ground. But the pit must be large enough for you to work in, and flooding is a danger. Installing the pump and filter above ground at a distance from the pool is easier.

Using the Terrace Pool

Owners of swimming pools should always regulate pool use so they are not victimized by neighbors, relatives, friends and total strangers. But if you have a pool in the terrace, the rules must be extra strict and enforced to the letter; otherwise you won't be able to use the terrace when you want to because the pool will be overloaded with the kids from next door. But I draw the line at giving advice about the content of the rules. That's a personal matter which you alone can settle. Enough to repeat that you must make the rules tough and enforce them in the same way.

130

11 Building Decks

Decks make it possible to live outdoors on a hillside. That is their principal reason for being. But they also enable you to build an outdoor room:

On top of rocks which are too large to remove;

At the second-floor level or any other level of the house so you can take better advantage of a view or to make the deck more accessible;

Around trees which might be killed if surrounded by a masonry terrace;

Bridging a stream or tiny picturesque valley;

Out over a pond;

On filled land which might not support a terrace;

On a beach where blowing and drifting sand would be a nuisance on a terrace.

Planning a Deck   Decks are categorized as low-level and high-level decks. The low-level type, obviously, is low to the ground and is hard to justify in situations where you can perfectly easily build a terrace and where a terrace has no drawbacks. The reason for this is that a deck is less attractive and less durable than a terrace, and it may very well be just as expensive. On the other hand, you can make a good case for low-level decks in situations like some of those cited in the preceding paragraphs.

However, there are no ifs, ands or buts about the value of a high-level deck because the only possible substitute for it is a wooden porch; and when you get right down to cases, there are no real differences between decks and porches.

Regardless of whether a deck is high or low, it should be located, sized and shaped like a terrace. See chapters 1 and 2. But three additional points must be considered in arriving at the final design:

1. If you're building a deck on a steep hillside with houses below, you owe it to your neighbors and your personal pride to build the supporting framework as attractively as possible. A maze of timbers is not at all good-looking; and it isn't necessary if you increase the size of the timbers so you can eliminate some of them or if you support the deck on reinforced concrete piers or steel posts.

Big deck projecting out from a house on a precipitous hillside is oriented entirely to an enormous view of one of the country's most beautiful rivers. Bronze-tinted glass screens cut the glare from the sky and weathered deck boards. Jonathan Isleib, designer. (Right) From the prow of the same deck looking toward the house. Two sizable oaks coming up through the floor give shade.

2. A deck should never be built so low to the ground that you can't crawl underneath to rescue a new litter of puppies or kittens or to chase out a nest of skunks or vipers. I don't know why other people who have written about decks never mention this; but it shows a woeful ignorance of animals or perhaps no concern for them or for the owners of the decks.

3. Because decks must bear heavy loads, feel sturdy underfoot, resist wind and perhaps water, and conform to building codes, they must be designed and built with great care. Quite honestly, I am not at all sure you should undertake it yourself. But if you do, remember that overbuilding is wiser than underbuilding. Don't skimp on the sizes and numbers and spacings of the timbers you use. And don't skimp on the fastenings either.

An entrancing multilevel deck surrounded with three types of fence. John Matthias, landscape architect. (PHOTO BY ERNEST BRAUN FOR THE CALIFORNIA REDWOOD ASSOCIATION)

Because the ground falls off sharply to Long Island Sound, the designer of this modern house chose to build a deck at the first-floor level across the entire back of the house. For other pictures of the square structure at the end of the deck, see chapter 8.

On such rugged land, construction of a terrace would have been almost impossible, so the owner built a deck atop a massive rock outcrop.

Building Footings and Piers

To make a deck resistant to up, down and lateral movement, you must build it up from footings and piers which extend below the frost line or at least 2 ft. down in frost-free areas. These can be constructed in various ways, but are best made of poured concrete mixed to the proportions given in chapter 5.

Post for a high-level deck is securely anchored to the concrete pier by two heavy steel straps embedded in the pier. Some types of anchor are designed to raise the post above the pier about an inch. The terrace floor, laid on shifting sand, is held in place by a timber framework.

The footings are square slabs measuring 16 x 16 x 8 in. deep. As soon as the concrete has set, construct piers in the form of a blunt pyramid on top. The tops of the piers should extend 6 in. above ground level and should be at least 2 in. larger in both directions than the wood posts they support. You can build the forms of ¾-in. plywood which is greased on the inside so the concrete will not stick. If you use double-headed nails, the forms can be easily taken apart and pulled from the concrete when it hardens.

Set post anchors in the tops of the piers while pouring the concrete. These should be made of heavy galvanized steel. The best are designed so that the posts are raised about an inch above the piers as a safeguard against decay. The posts are held in the anchors with large bolts.

Building the Underpinnings of the Deck

Decks are usually designed for a live load of 40 lb. per square foot plus an additional 10 lb. for the weight of the materials. The sizes of the timbers used depends on the spaces and grade of the wood, the height of the deck, the distances to be spanned and the

134

Underpinnings of the first deck illustrated. The main support is provided by two big rectangular columns of poured reinforced concrete. These are sheathed with vertical board siding.

spacing between timbers. In selecting lumber, it is also important to think about its decay resistance. If you use redwood, specify all-heartwood redwood. If you use any other wood, it should be thoroughly impregnated with a wood preservative—preferably at a mill.

The following tables, taken from the U.S. Forest Service's handbook No. 432, "Construction Guides for Exposed Wood Decks," give the minimum sizes of timbers you should use. To understand the tables, two points must be clarified:

First, the understructure of a deck consists of vertical posts supporting horizontal beams which, in turn, support the floor (or deck) joists. Unless a terrace is quite narrow, several parallel rows of beams are usually required; and this means that there must be several rows of posts.

Built high up in the treetops, this deck is supported by a concrete column and triangular steel braces bolted to the house framing and then covered with redwood boards to match the siding.

135

Table 1. Minimum Post Sizes
(Wood Beam Supports)[1]

Species group[2]	Post size (in.)	Load area[3] beam spacing x post spacing (sq. ft.)									
		36	48	60	72	84	96	108	120	132	144
1	4x4	Up to 12-ft. heights →					Up to 10-ft. heights →		Up to 8-ft. heights →		
	4x6		Up to 12-ft. heights →							Up to 10-ft. →	
	6x6							Up to 12-ft. →			
2	4x4	Up to 10-ft. hts. →					Up to 8-ft. heights →				
	4x6	Up to 12-ft. hts. →						Up to 10-ft. heights →			
	6x6							Up to 12-ft. heights →			
3	4x4	Up to 12' →	Up to 10' →		Up to 8-ft. hts. →			Up to 6-ft. heights →			
	4x6		Up to 12' →		Up to 10-ft. hts. →			Up to 8-ft. heights →			
	6x6				Up to 12-ft. heights →						

[1] Based on 40 p.s.f. deck live load plus 10 p.s.f. dead load. Grade is Standard and Better for 4- x 4-inch posts and No. 1 and Better for larger sizes.

[2] Group 1—Douglas-fir-larch and southern pine; Group 2—Hem-fir and Douglas-fir south; Group 3—Western pines and cedars, redwood, and spruces.

[3] Example: If the beam supports are spaced 8 feet, 6 inches, on center and the posts are 11 feet, 6 inches on center, then the load area is 98. Use next larger area 108.

136

Table 2. Minimum Beam Sizes and Spans[1]

Species group[2]	Beam size (in.)	Spacing between beams[3] (ft.)								
		4	**5**	**6**	**7**	**8**	**9**	**10**	**11**	**12**
1	4x6	Up to 6-ft. spans →								
	3x8	Up to 8-ft. →	Up to 7' →	Up to 6-ft. spans →						
	4x8	Up to 10' →	Up to 9' →	Up to 8' →	Up to 7-ft. →	Up to 6-ft. spans →				
	3x10	Up to 11' →	Up to 10' →	Up to 9' →	Up to 8' →	Up to 7-ft. →	Up to 6-ft. spans →			
	4x10	Up to 12' →	Up to 11' →	Up to 10' →	Up to 9' →	Up to 8-ft. →	Up to 7-ft. →	Up to 6-ft. →		
	3x12		Up to 12' →	Up to 11' →	Up to 10' →	Up to 9-ft. →	Up to 8-ft. spans →			
	4x12			Up to 12-ft. →	Up to 11' →	Up to 10' →	Up to 9-ft. spans →			
	6x10				Up to 12' →	Up to 11' →	Up to 10-ft. →	Up to 9-ft. spans →		
	6x12						Up to 12-ft. spans →			
2	4x6	Up to 6-ft. →								
	3x8	Up to 7-ft. →	Up to 6-ft. →							
	4x8	Up to 9' →	Up to 8' →	Up to 7-ft. →	Up to 6-ft. spans →					Up to 6' →
	3x10	Up to 10' →	Up to 9' →	Up to 8' →	Up to 7-ft. →	Up to 6-ft. spans →				
	4x10	Up to 11' →	Up to 10' →	Up to 9' →	Up to 8' →	Up to 7-ft. spans →		Up to 7-ft. spans →		
	3x12	Up to 12' →	Up to 11' →	Up to 10' →	Up to 9' →	Up to 8-ft. →	Up to 8-ft. →	Up to 7-ft. →		
	4x12		Up to 12' →	Up to 11' →	Up to 10' →	Up to 9' →	Up to 9-ft. spans →		Up to 8-ft. →	
	6x10			Up to 12' →	Up to 11' →	Up to 10-ft. →	Up to 9-ft. spans →		Up to 9-ft. spans →	
	6x12					Up to 12-ft. spans →		Up to 11-ft. →	Up to 11-ft. spans →	
3	4x6	Up to 6' →								
	3x8	Up to 7' →	Up to 6' →							
	4x8	Up to 8' →	Up to 7' →	Up to 6-ft. →						
	3x10	Up to 9' →	Up to 8' →	Up to 7' →	Up to 6-ft. spans →					
	4x10	Up to 10' →	Up to 9' →	Up to 8' →	Up to 7' →	Up to 6-ft. spans →		Up to 6-ft. spans →		
	3x12	Up to 11' →	Up to 10' →	Up to 9' →	Up to 8' →	Up to 7-ft. spans →		Up to 6-ft. →		
	4x12	Up to 12' →	Up to 11' →	Up to 10' →	Up to 9-ft. →	Up to 8-ft. →	Up to 8-ft. →	Up to 7-ft. →		
	6x10		Up to 12' →	Up to 11' →	Up to 10' →	Up to 9-ft. →	Up to 9-ft. spans →	Up to 8-ft. spans →		
	6x12			Up to 12-ft. →	Up to 11' →	Up to 11-ft. →	Up to 10-ft. →	Up to 10-ft. →		Up to 8' →

[1] Beams are on edge. Spans are center to center distances between posts or supports. (Based on 40 p.s.f. deck live load plus 10 p.s.f. dead load. Grade is No. 2 or Better; No. 2, medium grain southern pine.)

[2] Group 1—Douglas fir-larch and southern pine; Group 2—Hem-fir and Douglas-fir south; Group 3—Western pines and cedars, redwood, and spruces.

[3] Example: If the beams are 9 feet, 8 inches apart and the species is Group 2, use the 10-ft. column; 3x10 up to 6-ft. spans, 4x10 or 3x12 up to 7-ft. spans, 4x12 or 6x10 up to 9-ft. spans, 6x12 up to 11-ft. spans.

137

Table 3. Maximum Allowable Spans for Deck Joists[1]

Species group[2]	Joist size (inches)	Joist spacing (inches)		
		16	24	32
1	2x6	9'-9"	7'-11"	6'-2"
	2x8	12'-10"	10'-6"	8'-1"
	2x10	16'-5"	13'-4"	10'-4"
2	2x6	8'-7"	7'-0"	5'-8"
	2x8	11'-4"	9'-3"	7'-6"
	2x10	14'-6"	11'-10"	9'-6"
3	2x6	7'-9"	6'-2"	5'-0"
	2x8	10'-2"	8'-1"	6'-8"
	2x10	13'-0"	10'-4"	8'-6"

[1] Joists are on edge. Spans are center to center distances between beams or supports. Based on 40 p.s.f. deck live loads plus 10 p.s.f. dead load. Grade is No. 2 or Better; No. 2 medium grain southern pine.

[2] Group 1—Douglas-fir-larch and southern pine; Group 2—Hem-fir and Douglas-fir south; Group 3—Western pines and cedars, redwood, and spruces.

Second, the large numbers shown in the tables refer to the groups to which several wood species belong. Group 1, which is made up of the strongest wood species, includes Douglas fir, southern pine and western larch. In group 2 are western hemlock and white fir. In group 3 are redwood, spruces, white pines and cedars.

The tables are designed to help you find the proper timber sizes

Table 4. Maximum Allowable Spans for Spaced Deck Boards[1]

Species group[2]	Maximum allowable span (inches)[3]					
	Laid flat				Laid on edge	
	1 x 4	2 x 2	2 x 3	2 x 4	2 x 3	2 x 4
1	16	60	60	60	90	144
2	14	48	48	48	78	120
3	12	42	42	42	66	108

[1] These spans are based on the assumption that more than one floor board carries normal loads. If concentrated loads are a rule, spans should be reduced accordingly.

[2] Group 1—Douglas-fir-larch and southern pine; Group 2—Hem-fir and Douglas-fir south; Group 3—Western pines and cedars, redwood, and spruces.

[3] Based on Construction grade or Better (Select Structural, Appearance, No. 1 or No. 2).

once you know how the deck is to be constructed. That is, if your design calls for posts 10 ft. apart and beams 6 ft. apart, a glance at table 2 will show that your beams should measure at least 4 x 10 in. if made of group 1 wood; 3 x 12 in. if made of a group 2 wood; or 4 x 12 in. if made of a group 3 wood.

But how do you use the tables if you don't know the construction of the deck? Let's suppose you want to build a 10 x 20-ft. deck 8 ft. off the ground; and you want to space the posts 10 ft. apart along the length of the deck and space the beams 5 ft. apart. (In other words, you want three 20-ft.-long rows of posts each with three posts, over which you will place three 20-ft.-long rows of beams.)

Start with table 1 to find your posts. First determine the load area by multiplying 5 ft. times 10 ft. This gives a load area of 50 sq. ft., which should be increased to 60 sq. ft. The table shows you can use any 4 x 4-in. timbers for the posts.

Now move to table 2. This shows that with your desired 5-ft. spacing between beams, you must use a 3 x 10-in. timber of group 1 species to span posts spaced 10 ft. apart. The alternative is to use a 4 x 10 in group 2 or a 3 x 12 in group 3.

Table 3 tells you what joists to lay across the beams. Here you find that 2 x 6s of all species groups are adequate even if you space the joists 32 in. apart.

Table 4 covers deck boards which are spaced ¼ in. apart.

A half-lap joint at left; one-third-two-thirds lap joint at right.

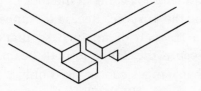

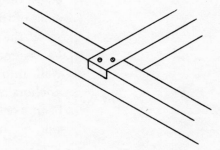

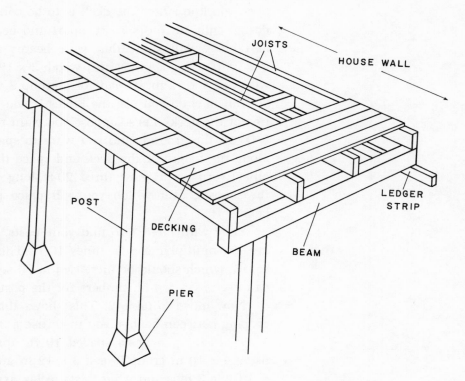

One way to frame a deck.

Because of the 32-in. joist spacing, ordinary 1-in.-thick boards are unacceptable. You must use 2-in. timbers.

Secure fastening of all timbers is essential. Use galvanized steel only.

To attach the beams to the tops of posts, use sheet-metal flanges made for the purpose. Recess the upper leaves into the sides of the beams a fraction of an inch so that moisture cannot get behind them. Secure the flange to both beam and post with 2½-in. nails. (Note that flanges can be used only if the beams and posts are the same thickness. If the beam is thinner than the post, align the edges on one side of the post and nail a large vertical cleat to the sides of the post and beam.)

If the deck is connected to the house, the beams or joists should be fastened to a ledger strip which is in turn fastened through the wall into the studs with spikes. On a masonry wall, use lead anchors and lag screws. For the ledger, use a 2 x 4-in. timber if the beams or joists rest on it; but if the beams or joists are hung at the side of the ledger, use a timber the same width as the beams or joists.

140

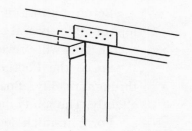

A steel flange is used to tie a beam to a post securely.

Joists can be set on top of beams (and a ledger strip) or held at the sides in U-shaped steel hangers. The former arrangement is slightly the stronger and permits you to extend the joists a couple of feet beyond the outer beams. Fasten the joists to the beams by toenailing with spikes, or use metal framing anchors. Hanging joists at the sides of the beams conceals the ends of the joists and thus gives the deck a somewhat more finished appearance around the sides.

If joists are made of 2 x 8s or wider timbers, install bridging between them at 10-ft. intervals to stiffen the floor. You can make the bridging of two 3-in. boards nailed in an X between each pair of joists, or of short lengths of joist lumber nailed between joists.

A deck attached to a house does not usually require bracing. But if it is distant from the house and more than 5 ft. high, install diagonal braces between the top of one post and the bottom of the next. Arrange the braces in a W pattern; don't let them all run in the same direction. Use 2 x 4s for braces under 8 ft.; 2 x 6s otherwise. Use lag screws or bolts to secure them.

On a free-standing deck between 3 and 5 ft. high, bracing is done by connecting each post to the beam with short 2 x 4s arranged in a V. Attach the braces to the posts 2 ft. below the beams; and attach them to the beam 2 ft. to either side of the posts.

A steel joist hanger is used to attach one timber to the side of a second timber.

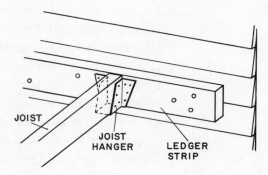

JOIST

JOIST HANGER

LEDGER STRIP

Before putting down floorboards, it is a good idea to cover the tops of all joists and beams with narrow strips of aluminum flashing metal. This will prevent water from standing on the wood.

Space the floorboards ⅛ to ¼ in. apart so water will drip through readily. Boards laid end to end should also be spaced slightly. The joints must be made over the center of a joist or beam.

For 2-in.-thick deck boards laid flat, use 3¼-in. galvanized nails of the annular-ring variety. Drive two nails at each joist. For appearance's sake, take pains to drive nails in a straight line across the deck.

Deck boards made from 2 x 3s may also be laid on edge. Use 5-in. nails—one per joist.

Prefabricated units for flooring terraces are also available. These have a general resemblance to the pallets used for shipping large machines. Three-foot squares are made with ten 2 x 4s nailed to three cleats made of 2 x 4s. Four-foot squares have 13 2 x 4s nailed to cleats. The pallets are designed with lips at the sides so that one helps to support the other when laid out on the deck framework. Adjacent pallets are laid with the floor boards perpendicular to each other, as in a parquet floor.

Railings and Benches   You would probably get into an argument with the National Safety Council if you built any deck, no matter how high, without some sort of railing or bench around the elevated sides. I'm not going to be as adamant as the Council, but I must point out that you can break a leg or arm or neck falling from a 3-in. height as easily as you can falling from 10 ft.

To give a railing or bench maximum strength, extend the posts above the deck floor and bolt the beams to their sides rather than across the tops. But you can build ample strength into a railing if you make the posts for it of 2 x 3-in. timbers and bolt them edgewise to the sides of the beams and/or joists. Space the posts 4 to 6 ft. apart and nail 2 x 3s to the inner surfaces to form the rails. Nail a flat cap board over the top rail and top of the posts to hasten water runoff and particularly to prevent water from settling into the end grain of the posts.

Railings can also be built with galvanized steel pipes as on a boat. Several designs are pictured.

On a very low deck, a simple bench without a back can take the place of a railing and provide seating space as well. The photograph on page 147 shows how it can be built with short seat posts made of

142

This fragile-looking railing is made of taut stainless-steel wires threaded through 3-in. steel pipes which are bolted to the joists beneath the floor.

*Built on Nantucket's
sand dunes, this low-level
deck is firmly anchored
against wind and water by
the huge posts coming up
through the floor to
support the benches.*

Handsome, specially fabricated railing is made of sturdy steel frames with stainless steel wires stretched between the legs.

4 x 4s bolted to the sides of the joists or beams. A pair of triangular 2 x 6s is bolted to the top of each post; and the bench top made of 2 x 6s is nailed to these.

The diagram on page 146 shows how to build a more comfortable bench with a back.

Design for a bench which also serves as a deck railing.

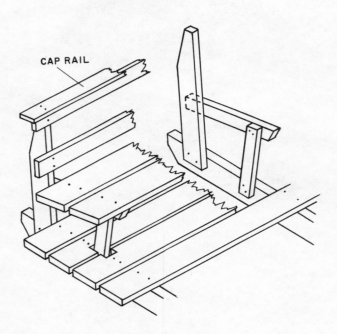

CAP RAIL

A simple bench around two sides of a deck. Wider than most (it's almost 24 in.), it's a good place for napping as well as sitting.

This house has a raised deck to permit enjoyment of an ocean view and a ground-level terrace for normal living. Strips and squares of canvas are used to ward off some of the wind blowing across the deck and give privacy for sunbathing.

Finishing a Deck   Don't use paint. It just doesn't wear well on a deck floor and needs to be refinished every couple of years at least.

The easiest finish is none at all. Let the sun and rain weather the wood to a lovely gray patina. As pointed out in chapter 5, if the natural weathering process seems too slow, apply a bleaching stain to the new wood. This turns the wood gray immediately. When the stain finally wears away, nature will have taken over.

To retain the original color of wood, apply a water repellent— a colorless liquid which not only interferes with natural weathering but also helps to prevent splitting and checking of wood. And if it contains a mildewcide, it also stops formation of mildew. Use two coats as a starter. In arid regions you may never need another. Elsewhere, when you notice the wood starting to darken, apply a new coat or, if you decide to change the color apply one or two coats of an exterior oil stain.

Oil stains can also be used on brand new decks if you want to retain the texture of the wood but change the color to green, blue, gray—you name it. Use two coats and apply the second within 30 minutes of the first. This lengthens the life of the stain substantially. But eventually the color will fade and a new coat will be needed.

12 Atriums

Since an atrium is completely surrounded by the house, it is almost always planned along with the house. Rarely does the owner of an existing house build an atrium by knocking a hole in the center or by wrapping a new wing around the terrace.

Atriums (the word was first used by the ancient Romans to describe the magnificent interior terraces and gardens built by wealthy home owners) are entrancing because they are truly one with the house. If you take my description of terraces as outdoor rooms with a grain of salt, you can omit the salt when I refer to an atrium as an outdoor room, because a room it is—no question about it. You can enter it from the rooms on every side; walk through it when going from, say, the living room to your bedroom.

It brings the outdoors into every room that overlooks it, gives complete privacy from the world, is largely free of wind and serves as a warm, sunny oasis the year round.

The fact that atriums are—and have always been—more common in warm climates than cold is no accident. The sun is more directly overhead; consequently, it reaches into all corners of the atrium. This, in turn, means that if you surround an atrium in the south with a two-story house, it will receive almost wall-to-wall light. In the north, however, you should build an atrium only in a one-story house so the walls will not keep the slanting rays of the sun from the north side of the atrium.

Most atriums are open to the sky. If you want protection from rain, the easiest way to provide it is by extending the roof overhangs. But for a price, you can have the entire atrium roofed with glass by a firm specializing in such structures.

If screening proves necessary (it may not), rolling out screen wire on a network of heavy supporting wires should give adequate protection even though the joints between strips are merely overlapped, not sealed.

Paving for the atrium must be selected with unusual care because of the surrounding walls. If it is too light in color, the glare spreads into the house; if it's too dark, the soaked-up heat spreads into the house. Wood blocks, bricks and AstroTurf are especially good choices.

If the atrium is unroofed, several large drains must be installed in the paving and connected into 4- to 6-in. pipes leading away from the house. In areas with heavy soil, put a 6 to 12-in. layer of gravel or crushed rock under planting beds; and if the soil is extremely dense, install perforated drainpipes in the gravel to collect water and lead it away from the house.

13 Gazebos and Garden Houses

A gazebo can be—and very often is—the most charming element of a garden. This is because its purpose is more ornamental than practical; so it is designed to be an art work and is placed where you can enjoy it to your heart's content. This doesn't mean it is always in a prominent position. The exceptionally beautiful gazebo on this page, for example, is tucked off so that you come on it almost accidentally. But when you do find it, you can't take your eyes off it and you are drawn to it to relax on its marble base and feast on the colors of the dogwoods and azaleas surrounding it.

Gazebos are never large. I think the average wouldn't seat more than four persons. They're *usually* round, hexagonal or octagonal; open at the sides and top; and raised only a few inches off the ground. But don't consider these rules to abide by. That's one of the charms of the little structures. Like sculpture, no two should be alike.

Most gazebos are pretty; this one is extraordinary. Stanley Underhill, landscape architect.

This gazebo overlooking the Pacific Ocean is a blend of modern and Oriental design. The humpy planting below it is a form of zoysia grass.

Garden houses are just as variable, but they are more architectural than sculptural. And they are larger. As a result, they don't have quite the charm of gazebos but they are more usable by more people.

Again there are no rules about design or construction. Most of the structures that I think of as garden houses are at least partially open at the sides (but rarely at the top) at all times of the year. But a garden house which can be completely enclosed (though not permanently) offers one advantage: it can be used for storage of terrace furniture under cover and out of sight in winter. This is a problem for most homeowners.

152

(Top) *I'm not sure whether this is a gazebo or garden house. It is made of steel mesh and is suggestive of a Saracen's tent.*

(Center) *Unusually large garden house with storage and work space at right and a lathhouse for tropical and shade-loving plants at left. The open living area back of the awning faces a vast flower garden.*

(Bottom, left) *To add to the interest of this charming gazebo, the owner keeps a pair of fantail pigeons in a cage inside. Ivy is trained on the garden wall to carry out the design of the gazebo.*

(Right) *A Philadelphia-area garden house built like a Japanese teahouse. The large roof offers ample protection against rain although the house is open in front and on the sides. The back wall is made of translucent plastic. Frederick W. G. Peck, landscape architect.*

This garden house is
separated from the main
house, which it faces,
by a triangular lawn and
planting area given over to
bulbs and perennials.
Part of the structure is used
for storage.

A belvedere—an old British form of garden house— overlooks this formal garden in the heart of old Philadelphia.

One thing to remember if you build a garden house is that you must get a building permit before you start. It probably would be a good idea also to inquire whether you need a permit for a gazebo. Both should be built within the setback lines required by your town's zoning code.

14 Furnishing the Terrace

Twice recently I have run across peacock chairs on terraces; and both times they gave me a turn because I recall so well the peacock chair on my parents' terrace in Haverford, Pennsylvania. Not that it played any part whatever in my life. It was just beautiful. In those days it spoke of the mysterious Orient. Today it's nostalgic. But it is still the handsomest piece of terrace furniture you can buy.

That's saying something, because in the past ten or fifteen years terrace furniture has taken giant steps forward in appearance and practicality. Most of the best lines are made of painted aluminum or sometimes steel with vinyl webbing. Though of modern design, they are suitable to any style of terrace; comfortable; very durable; fairly easy to maintain. The only thing that bothers me is that there is a great sameness to the pieces and they cost a lot.

Exactly the same comments can be made about the other furniture sold by the same manufacturers. Here the vinyl webbing is replaced either by springy metal strapping or plastic-foam cushions covered with a variety of natural and synthetic fabrics.

Ornamental cast-iron chairs, benches and tables—now usually duplicated (but not so well) in cast aluminum—continue to pop up on terraces all across the land. I asked Elizabeth why, because the stuff is terribly uncomfortable, and she opined that it looks luxurious to many people. And I guess it does. But it should be used only to look at or perhaps for momentary perching. I saw some the other day at the end of a lawn above Lake Erie. It helped to make a very pretty and inviting picture. But it was interesting to note that the owners of the property evidently didn't think much of its comfort because they didn't have anything like it on their terrace.

If you want really comfortable furniture with the somewhat rococo look of the old-style cast-metal pieces, it's easy enough to come by—at a price. Most of the big terrace-furniture makers turn it out. The slender framework is made of extruded aluminum or wrought iron. The chairs, benches and chaises have cushions of plastic foam covered with water-resistant fabric. The tabletops are glass.

Solid-plastic furniture is slow to make headway despite the fact that plastics are more weather-resistant than other materials. Chairs

There is no more need to furnish a terrace all in one style than there is to furnish a living room that way. But the pieces should go together. On this terrace the owners use two different but similar styles of metal furniture. Even greater diversity is apparent in some of the other terraces pictured.

*Swinging basket chairs
are fun and comfortable—
especially if you're young.
A simple hexagonal bench
surrounds the maple tree.*

molded in one piece of rigid plastic are too severely modern for most tastes, and sitting on them is like sitting on a board. But when the framework alone is made of plastic and the seat is webbed or cushioned, both appearance and comfort are greatly increased. So, alas, is the price.

Rattan and wicker furniture is as charming as ever and a lot more comfortable than it was in its heyday in the twenties. But it suffers from two serious drawbacks: it's hard to maintain, and it's miserable to refinish.

There isn't much else in ready-made furniture that deserves a place on the terrace even though it is comparatively low in cost.

160

Folding aluminum chairs and chaises with plastic webbing are an abomination. Solid wood is too cumbersome. Captain's chairs (or director's chairs) and other canvas-covered pieces are too hard to keep up.

Selecting Furniture for the Terrace

I leave the very important matter of design up to you. You know what you like and what is most suitable for your terrace. But practical matters must be taken into consideration.

How easy is the furniture to maintain? Rattan, wicker and canvas are hopeless. They collect dirt and cling to it as if it were magnetized.

If wood is painted, it needs to be refinished about every other year. If varnished or finished with some other hard, transparent protective coating, it needs to be refinished annually because no finish of this kind can withstand the sun. If not finished, it stains badly.

Cast iron and steel also need frequent repainting even though some new terrace furniture has joints sealed against the weather. Chrome-plated steel, on the other hand, needs very little maintenance—in fact, less than any material used in terrace furniture except unpeeled cedar logs.

Unfinished aluminum is used only in the cheapest furniture and corrodes so badly that you eventually throw it out or coat it with paint which doesn't stick. Aluminum with a factory-applied baked-enamel finish is much more trouble-free. This is not to say that the finish resists scratching; but in my experience, it lasts very well.

Solid plastic is also durable; but except for plastics which are reinforced with fiberglass, the material scratches rather easily. And when the surface becomes a maze of scratches, there's nothing you can do to improve it.

Plastic webbing is considerably less desirable. Vinyl is the only type which can be called durable; but it soils badly and is not very easy to clean. Of the webbings made of woven plastic filaments, saran is the only one I have yet found which can survive more than a year or two of exposure to the weather. Polypropylene—the material used in cheap furniture—isn't much better than cheesecloth.

To what extent will the furniture be exposed to wind? In our former house, the wind sweeping across the meadow frequently tossed our lightweight aluminum-and-vinyl furniture around like tumbleweeds. Friends with a high deck above the Connecticut River

161

Even on a terrace as well protected as this, an umbrella must either be firmly anchored or weighted to keep winds from carrying it away.

report that their heavier steel-and-vinyl furniture has received the same treatment. On several occasions, indeed, chairs have been tossed right over the railing onto rocks and shrubs 50 ft. below. It's a wonder that they were not thrown against or through the glass doors opening onto the deck.

These may be extreme cases, but they are not rare. If your terrace is exposed to occasional hard winds, you should either buy furniture that is heavy enough to resist movement by everything except a tornado, or screen the terrace against the blast. And even if your terrace isn't windswept, you must be careful when buying an umbrella table to make sure that the umbrella can be easily collapsed when not in use and is well weighted down or anchored at all times.

Will the furniture be easy to store? Of course, you may just leave it on the terrace the year round. (More on this later.) If not, the ease with which you can store it must be considered. Three questions should be raised:

Is it too heavy to carry from the terrace to the storage place and back again?

Is it too large to be carried through the storeroom door?

Can it be folded up or stacked for storage in a small space?

How safe and maintenance-free are glass tabletops? From the safety standpoint, only tempered safety glass should be used because, if broken, it disintegrates into small, harmless pellets. From the maintenance standpoint, frosted glass is preferable to clear because it does not show dirt to the same extent; and if the table rim on which it rests gets grimy—as it almost always does—the glass conceals the dirt pretty well.

Building Your Own Terrace Furniture

Most homemade terrace furniture looks like what it is: a flimsy, unattractive replica of the old-fashioned Adirondack chair. It has no place on your beautiful terrace.

Unless you have a real feel for furniture design and the specialized tools to translate plans into realities, don't venture beyond the following simple pieces:

CABLE REEL TABLE This is suitable for only the simplest or most rustic terrace—which is unfortunate because absolutely anyone can create it. All you have to do is pay a visit to your electric utility's construction department and ask if you can have one of the smaller wooden reels on which cable is shipped.

164

*No great thing of beauty,
but it's a useful table
and cost not a cent: an old
cable reel.*

When you get the reel home, you can just put it out on the terrace and let it weather. But you will improve its appearance somewhat if you fasten loose parts together with galvanized nails or screws; then sand the reel as smooth as possible; and finish it with a couple of coats of oil stain or exterior alkyd paint.

Though crude, the reels make excellent tables which cannot be blown over or away by a hurricane.

FLAGSTONE COFFEE TABLE   This is not suitable for a formal terrace; but it is very handsome, sturdy and permanent. Its major flaw is that if you run into it on a dark night, your shinbone will develop a knob the size of your nose. And if you build it with a central pedestal, sooner or later some joker will sit on the edge and break off the top (but it can be put back in short order).

Make the tabletop of flagstone or slate. You can use whatever you find in a masonry-supply yard or have a top cut to whatever size and shape you like.

If the top is not extremely large, it can be supported on a central pedestal made of a single concrete block set on end; an 8 x 8-in. pier of bricks cemented together; or a large rock. Anchor the top to the pedestal with ½-in. thickness of concrete made of 1 part Portland cement and 2½ parts sand.

For a large table, or to build a small table which cannot be broken by a table-edge sitter, put legs under the four corners. These are easily made of bricks laid up with cement to form piers measuring 4 x 8 in. by whatever height you like.

PERMANENT BENCH   Two benches for decks are illustrated in chapter 11. To build a permanent bench without a back on a masonry terrace, use 4 x 4-in. timbers for legs and set them in the ground to a depth of 12 to 18 in. Rest the bottom ends on a thick bed of gravel and surround them with concrete. Bolt crosspieces to the tops of the posts as in the picture on page 140 and nail the top to these. The bench can be about 16 in. high or a little more. Make the top 15 to 24 in. wide. Space the supports about 6 ft. apart.

Although it saves lumber to make the bench top of 2 x 6s laid flat, narrow timbers spaced ⅛ to ¼ in. apart make a better-looking top and do not cup or warp as much. Use 2 x 3s installed on edge or flat.

PORTABLE BENCH   The simplest bench is essentially the same as the above. Use 2 x 12s about 14 in. high for the legs. Out of a 2 x 3, cut cleats 1 in. less than the bench width and nail these to the sides of the legs flush with the tops. Then nail the boards forming the bench top to the cleats. To keep the legs from wobbling brace them with angle irons screwed to the underside of the top.

A more graceful bench is made with steel legs, which must be fabricated in a metalworking shop. The legs are made of ¼ x 4-in. steel bars bent in the form of a W. At the top, the W should be 1 to 1¼ in. less than the bench width; at the bottom it should be 3 to 4 in. less than the bench width. The inverted V in the center of the W should be only about 2 in. high.

Fasten 2 x 4-in. timbers between the top edges of the W and flush with them. Nail or screw the bench top to the timbers.

**Storing
Terrace Furniture**

Even though it is unused, a terrace in winter should be attractive when you look out at it. That means it should be devoid of furniture, because nothing looks more desolate than a terrace scattered with chairs without cushions and tables without tops. And if there's anything pleasant about a huge mound of furniture covered with a tired tarpaulin, I don't know what it is.

But how in the world can anyone clear his terrace of furniture if he doesn't have anyplace to store it? That's the big question, and I don't have a ready answer.

I'm lucky because we have a barn which can absorb everything; and in our former house we had a basement almost as capacious. But Elizabeth's cousin Harry built his house without basement, attic or any other large storage space except the garage, which isn't big enough for automobiles plus terrace furniture plus the countless other things most people store in garages.

Harry is not the only one in this fix.

Using folding and deflatable furniture is not an answer to the problem because, while it saves space in storage, it adds little to the beauty of the terrace in summer. And anyway it is surprisingly bulky even when folded.

Short of building a storage shed for the furniture—and I don't think much of that because most sheds are pretty ugly—I have only a few suggestions to offer:

1. Buy furniture which will be suitable for use indoors in the family room, breakfast room, etc., in winter.

2. Buy furniture from a dealer who will store it for you while he reconditions it. This isn't a cheap proposition, admittedly. The store that sold us some of our aluminum-and-vinyl furniture charges

The season is late and the cushions have been removed from a double chaise. But the chaise will remain on the terrace for possible occupancy until Indian summer comes and goes.

one half of the original cost of each piece for annual refurbishing and storage. But besides avoiding the storage problem, you start out with furniture in mint-new condition every spring.

3. Build a storage rack in the garage over the hood of your car. You'll be amazed how much stuff you can store on it even though you leave 6-ft. headroom underneath.

4. Build a storage room under a deck which is elevated more than about 3 ft. (But the deck floor must be made solid or you must build a roof over the storage area to keep the furniture dry.)

5. If permanent benches are built on the terrace, turn the space under the seats into watertight chests for cushions and other small items.

Maintaining and Repairing Terrace Furniture

All furniture which can be damaged by rain should either be moved under a roof when the terrace is not in use or covered. Covering is easier, obviously; but not cheap. Fitted vinyl covers for chairs start at $7; for a large wooden chaise, you'll pay $10. But table covers are cheaper because you don't need anything more than a vinyl tablecloth or a good-looking shower curtain.

UNFINISHED ALUMINUM   You can help to prevent the aluminum from corroding by applying two coats of methacrylate lacquer after the first year, and applying a single new coat every couple of years thereafter. Otherwise, clean the metal several times a year with naval jelly.

PAINTED ALUMINUM   This requires little attention—just an occasional wipe with a damp cloth—until it becomes scratched. Then you should touch it up with any good enamel made for use on metal.

IRON AND STEEL   Examine this furniture every spring for loose paint and rust. Remove any defects you find by scraping with a knife or coarse file until the metal is bright. Sand well. Then prime with a red lead primer and follow with one or two coats of metal enamel.

Even though an old paint film is sound, repainting every two years is a good safeguard against rusting.

WOOD   Avoid constant exposure to the weather since sun and rain combine to make wood crack. A gloss enamel protects wood best but usually needs to be reapplied every two years. Don't use a hard transparent coating such as varnish if you like natural wood. You'll have less maintenance if you leave the wood unfinished or apply a water repellent or penetrating sealer. Wood handled in this way, however, is easily stained by foods, grease, etc.

Reglue loose joints as you find them with resorcinol glue. Fill cracks with plastic wood if the furniture is unfinished; use exterior spackle or wood putty on painted wood.

RATTAN AND WICKER   Wash frequently with detergent solution and a hard spray to keep dirt from permanently clogging the joints and interstices. Repaint painted furniture every two or three years. Use urethane varnish on natural-finished furniture, but don't expose the pieces to the sun. The varnish should be reapplied annually.

If bindings break, reglue them at once with epoxy or clear cellulose glue, and drive small copper nails through the ends.

CANVAS   To keep canvas clean you must wash it two or three times every summer in a strong detergent solution. Use bleach on white canvas. Even so, don't expect to keep the canvas in presentable condition for more than a couple of years. Before storing for the winter, wash and dry thoroughly. Then roll it up in plastic film.

WEBBING   Solid vinyl webbing seems to last almost indefinitely but needs frequent cleaning with a strong detergent solution of special vinyl cleaner.

Woven webbing also needs frequent washing; but don't count on its surviving many years of use. When a few strips start to disintegrate, replace all the webbing with new saran webbing. To do this, pull out the clips securing the webbing to the underside of the framework. Cut new strips to the same length, fold the ends into points and fasten the strips to the framework with aluminum sheet-metal screws. The screw threads must be slightly larger in diameter than the holes which held the clips.

15 Cooking on the Terrace

I've always been intrigued with the idea of building a kitchen on the terrace but I'll never do it because I'm not all that enthusiastic about outdoor cooking. Perhaps you feel differently; and if that's the case, here's all you have to do:

Under a roofed part of the terrace, probably against the wall of the house, build a closet 30 in. deep. Hang bifold doors on the front to seal it against the weather and to permit ready access to every corner when the doors are open. And then put in the appliances. The smallest "complete kitchen" unit on the market is only 30 in. wide and 36 in. high. It incorporates a 5- or 6-cu.-ft. refrigerator, stainless steel sink and two gas or electric burners. For baking, you can mount a conventional or microwave oven on the wall above.

Other complete-kitchen units range upward in size to a monster of 90 in. which has everything, including a dishwasher. Or you can, of course, assemble a kitchen of your own design.

I'd use the smallest full-size refrigerator-freezer available because, even though you might not need it for cooking meals (unless you cook every dinner outdoors, in which case you would want to keep certain things such as eggs, milk and butter on hand at all times), you could certainly use it for storing soft drinks, beer, ice cream and ice for daily use.

The sink, made of stainless steel, should be no less than 20 in. wide so you can easily wash the grid for a large barbecue grill. I'd actually prefer a deep sink, like a laundry tray, because one of the main purposes of a terrace sink is to let you fill a watering can and soak potted plants. A garbage disposer in the sink drain is useful because it helps to get rid not only of food wastes but also dead flowers from the garden.

Whether you need a dishwasher depends on whether you use the terrace kitchen every day. If you do, it's easier to keep a set of dishes and glasses on the terrace; and that means a dishwasher would come in handy.

On the theory that terrace cookery is never quite as extensive or elaborate as that indoors, my choice in ranges is a 21-in.-wide apartment-house model. Because it lacks the fancy features of larger models, it is inexpensive yet does everything a range is supposed to do. There's adequate space for oven cooking and keeping things warm while you wait for the steak to get done on the barbecue. And you can have either three or four burners.

Space for storing utensils, etc., should be provided under the sink and on the wall above. A series of short shelves mounted on the same slotted standards which are used for bookcases gives excellent flexibility. Install a large fluorescent light on the ceiling just above the doors to illuminate the kitchen. No ventilation is required if the doors extend from the terrace floor to the roof; but if you put in shorter doors, thus creating a pocket at the top of the closet, you should install a small exhaust fan or simple louvered opening in the wall above the doors.

If such a setup sounds too fancy for even semiserious consideration, a useful but much simpler kitchen can be built around a small sink and a 2-cu.-ft. "portable" refrigerator. For cooking, use a hotplate and any other small appliances you favor.

Appliance Carts   With an appliance cart you can set up cooking operations on your terrace wherever it suits you; and when you're through, you can roll the dirty utensils and dishes back to the kitchen for washing. This at least is the theory of appliance carts. But the theory doesn't always work out in practice because the carts are not well designed.

I'm not going to suggest a design, because it's more fun to work out your own; and anyway, you're the only one who knows what your cart should include. If you want a plan, however, you can get detailed drawings for $1 from the American Plywood Association, 1119 A St., Tacoma, Washington 98104. But here are some practical points to take into consideration:

1. When not in use, an appliance cart must be parked somewhere; and since most houses are short of adequate parking space indoors, that somewhere will probably be on the terrace. It follows that there must be a way you can close the cart to keep out moisture. Your choice lies between an arrangement of built-in lids and doors or a fitted vinyl cover.

2. To roll the cart from the terrace into the house and back again, you must negotiate either a step or threshold. If it's a step, my recommendation is to forget the whole idea. If it's a threshold, you must equip the cart with wheels which are large enough to ride

over it smoothly and without great exertion on the pusher's part. Casters—even big casters—are no good because when they strike the threshold, they swivel sideways and the cart takes a nosedive. You need rubber-tired wheels comparable in size to those on a wheelbarrow.

3. If the cart is to carry a refrigerator, the refrigerator must be placed just above the axles to lower the cart's center of gravity; otherwise, no matter what wheels you use, the cart may turn over when you roll over the threshold and even when you roll across an uneven brick floor.

4. Equip the cart with handles on the bow as well as on the stern. It makes for greater maneuverability and allows two persons to lift the cart over the threshold when heavily loaded.

5. Provide ample rims around the top of the cart and all shelves to keep things from falling off.

6. If the cart carries more than one electrical appliance, install a multiple outlet box in it; and provide a single heavy-duty cord to bring power to the box from a built-in terrace outlet.

Portable Barbecue Grills

There are four things to think about when buying a portable grill:

1. Open braziers with a grid suspended above a steel bowl are suitable only for broiling and a limited amount of roasting. If a grill has an electrically driven rotisserie, roasting is improved. And if a grill has a tight-fitting, ventilated cover, you can use it for smoking and baking.

2. The charcoal flavor given to meat results not from a special ingredient in charcoal, but from smoke rising from grease dripping on hot fuel. For this reason, gas-fired and electric grills give the same flavor as real charcoal grills. In addition, they are much easier to start; and there is no fuel to store.

3. A tabletop grill is a good choice only if you have a heatproof, greaseproof, easily cleaned surface to set it on. You can use a roll-around grill anywhere. On the other hand, since a roll-around is much larger, it is harder to store.

4. Cheap grills are an abomination because they are shoddily built; roll-around models often topple over when you push them; and many of them are too unattractive to keep on the terrace when not in use.

Expensive grills are stronger, heavier, easier to move and better-looking. But if you don't keep them clean and protect them against corrosion, my New England ancestry says it's silly to put the extra money into them.

Permanent Barbecue Grills

The most popular type of permanent grill today is a heavily constructed rectangular covered unit mounted on an aluminum pedestal. It can burn electricity but usually burns natural gas, and therein lies its only advantage over a portable grill: if you're an enthusiastic user of natural gas, this is the only grill equipped to burn it.

The other type of permanent grill is one you build yourself out of brick, stone or concrete block. It has only two reasons for being: either you do a lot of entertaining and need more cooking surface than is afforded by a portable grill, or you want to use it also for heating the terrace. Like the new gas grills, however, masonry grills are a nuisance because, when the wind is blowing from the wrong direction, there's nothing you can do to keep them from smoking up the terrace. And you have to keep them clean if they are to be presentable; you can't just roll them away out of sight like a portable.

If you build a masonry grill, try to face the firebox toward the prevailing wind in order to secure the best draft. Protect it from strong winds, which might scatter sparks; and keep it out from under trees, which would be damaged by the rising heat.

The easiest kind of masonry grill to build is nothing more than a box which is open at the front and top. A grate to hold the fire is suspended above the hearth, and a second grate for the food is set above this and a few inches below the top rim. Such a fireplace has relatively little value as a heating plant, however, because it is usually narrow and deep; consequently the back does not radiate much heat from a log fire on to the terrace.

If you want a simple fireplace which serves both as a large cookstove and as a reasonably effective heating plant, it should have a firebox at least 2 ft. wide by 2 ft. deep by 3 ft. high.

No special base is required if the fireplace is built up from the terrace floor. Otherwise, excavate to a depth of 8 in.; pour in 4 in. of gravel or crushed rock; and pour a 4-in. concrete slab on top. The slab should be 2 to 4 in. wider and longer than the overall fireplace.

Unusual fireplace used strictly for barbecuing is well lighted by a large postlamp. The kitchen is just out of view to the right.

Make the slab of the same concrete mix used for wall footings (see chapter 5).

For a brick fireplace (which is about as easy to construct as one of concrete block, and considerably more attractive), use common bricks and stick them together with a mortar made of 1 part Portland cement, ¼ part hydrated lime and 3 parts sand.

On top of the slab, construct a hearth one brick thick. Then build the sides and back two tiers (two bricks) thick. Install the fire grate 26 in. above the top of the concrete slab (24 in. above the hearth); and make provision for placing the cooking grate 4, 6 and 8 in. higher. Both grates should be movable so you can take

175

them out when you build a log fire on the hearth for warmth. To provide for this, insert 3-in. bolts ¼ in. in diameter into the mortar joints and allow the heads to protrude into the firebox about 1 in.

This same kind of fireplace can be built in a semicircle or as half of a hexagon if you can find grates of suitable shape or if you build in permanent grates made of ⅝ in. steel reinforcing rods.

Whatever the design of a masonry fireplace or whatever the material going into it, don't be too eager to try it out. Cure the concrete for two weeks by sprinkling it regularly with water or keeping it covered with wet burlap.

16 Entertaining on the Terrace

Terrace entertaining is best of all entertaining because it's so care-free, casual and colorful. I think this is better reflected in the so-called shelter magazines—those dealing with houses and gardens —than anywhere else. The fall and winter issues are invariably dull and frequently addlepated to compensate for the dullness. But when spring comes the magazines suddenly turn lighthearted, gay and full of fun; and it's all because they are reporting what people are doing outdoors on their terraces to savor the enjoyment of life and nature and friends.

On an early spring day a bright sun brings luncheon guests thronging to the terrace to bask in the soporific warmth and drink in the freshness of greening grass, cloudless sky and daffodils blooming on a wooded hillside.

On a summer evening, idle suburban chitchat after a satisfying dinner is muted by the hiss and patter of a sudden shower.

And on a chilly autumn night everyone gathers together companionably to relish the aroma and warmth of a fire flickering in the terrace fireplace while watching the shooting stars chase one another across the heavens.

Yes, there's something special about terrace entertaining. But it's not my intention to give you twenty clever ideas for smashing terrace parties. I won't give you even one. Neither do I offer any recipes. Let the magazines provide those.

All I have is a few comments on how to get a little extra pleasure out of terrace entertaining.

Seating

Seating for everyone is a must if you are serving food that is eaten with forks and knives. Of course, it's equally essential indoors; but indoors the host frequently relies on a stairway to provide the seating places he is missing in his furniture. Generally, there are no stairs to fall back on outdoors, so for large parties you must either borrow or rent chairs or build a wall.

Low walls around the edges of terraces are great for parties. They may not have other value, but for seating you can't beat them. I'm not sure just what their magnetism is, but the next time you go to a party on a walled terrace, notice where people sit first. On the wall.

Tables Tables are not as necessary as chairs for eating off plates, but guests are a little happier when they have them. We seem to have gone in for small iron tables that come in nests of three; but there are other types of nesting unit. You can also use TV tables. Or you can take a tip from one family that uses tall, narrow peach baskets for auxiliary tables. Painted gay colors, the baskets are quite in keeping with the easygoing atmosphere of a terrace. And when the party's over, they can be stacked in a small space.

Plates and Glasses I am not sold on eating and drinking out of plastic—most certainly not out of that flimsy, cheap stuff everyone has been using lately for large cocktail parties. But on a terrace, I must say, expensive plastic dinnerware and insulated plastic glasses make sense because they usually don't break when dropped on the paving.

Napery Paper napkins and tablecloths are fine if a terrace is totally free of wind, but very annoying otherwise. Give your guests and the after-party clean-up crew a break—use cloth.

Music If you like it on the terrace, why not pipe it out there via a couple of built-in loudspeakers? Weather-resistant speakers are available.

Decorative Lighting Rigging up special lighting for an evening party is one of the happiest parts of throwing such a party.

I don't recall why, but Elizabeth and I started out years ago by putting small electric lights in Japanese lanterns, which we hung from the terrace roof. Then, after the lanterns became badly torn, we made a spur-of-the-moment shift to quart Mason jars wrapped in thin Christmas and birthday wrappings.

Still later, we discovered the charm of ordinary brown paper bags weighted with about 2 in. of sand and with a single large candle burning in the middle. Stationed around the edges of the terrace and throughout the garden, they gave a warm enchantment to the night.

Tall Hawaiian torches put out considerably more light and have a fascination of their own. Burning kerosene, they give off a flame that defies wind and rain. But place them carefully. If set on poles, be sure they are not under roofs and trees. If you use the heads alone, put them on the ground in big sand-filled flowerpots which won't readily tip over.

Other ways of lighting for a party are to use old-fashioned kerosene hand lamps of the type we must fall back on when there's a power outage.

Or scatter mosquito lights throughout the terrace and float them in the terrace pool.

Or surround the terrace with vigil lights.

17 Planting the Terrace

I've known terraces without any planting on or around them. Most had a spectacular view so you weren't terribly conscious of what was missing. But they had a cold severity, a certain drabness that made them feel vaguely uncomfortable.

Plants and terraces go together. Plants give a terrace warmth and oneness with the world and serve such useful functions as providing shade, privacy and protection against wind. Terraces, on the other hand, serve as a backdrop for the color and texture of plants and enable us to contemplate and enjoy the indescribable beauty of plants.

The planning of the terrace planting should be started when you plan the terrace itself. The following questions should be answered:

What practical purposes will the planting serve? Is it needed for shade? To screen out an undesirable view? To give privacy from neighbors? To break the wind? To take the place of a fence around the edges of a slightly raised terrace? To soak up water pouring off a house roof without gutters and keep it from flooding the terrace? To call attention to changes in elevation between multi-level terraces? To hold a bank below the terrace?

What are the esthetic purposes of the planting? To soften the lines of the terrace and/or house walls? To give the terrace color and texture? To create a pleasant outlook from the terrace? To frame a distant view? To "tie down" a raised terrace or to screen the underpinnings of a high-level deck? To separate the terrace floor from the house wall and thus eliminate a hard, ugly corner joint? To conceal to some extent a sizable difference in elevation between the terrace and house? To frame the terrace when you view it from across the yard? To outline the edges of a terrace which is level with the lawn? To break up a vast expanse of paving?

Are there existing plants which affect the size, shape, construction and planting of the terrace? Trees, for instance, very often dictate terrace design and planting.

Is there anything about the terrace which influences the selection and placement of plants? For example, as pointed out in chapter 4, if a terrace is paved with concrete masonry, you're likely to kill trees which are surrounded by the pavement. Similarly, if you build a terrace on the north side of the house, sun-loving plants cannot be planted next to the house wall because they will be in almost perpetual shade.

Which plants are suited to your climate? This is a crucial question, of course, because you can't expect to grow tropical plants in the North or most northern plants in the Deep South. But the answer is not hard to come by because any good local nurseryman can supply it. Or you need only consult the plant descriptions and map which follow. First, look at the map to determine in which climate zone you live. If it looks as if you live on the dividing line between two zones, assume for safety's sake that you live in the zone with the lower number.

Partially walled, partially screened terrace in Southern California appears almost solidly planted with white alyssum, pink begonias and a variety of shrubs and vines. The owner has painted a mural on the rear wall.

A beautiful arrangement of delightfully contrasting plants at the end of a long, narrow terrace. The star-shaped leaves of a sweet gum overhang the wall. The low Japanese yew is a permanent spot of dark green. The clump of gray birches is bright green and brings movement to the scene since the leaves dance in every breeze.

A simple but charming arrangement of plants and sculpture. The feathery plant is Japanese andromeda; the potted plant, schefflera.

Plant Hardiness Zone Map[1]

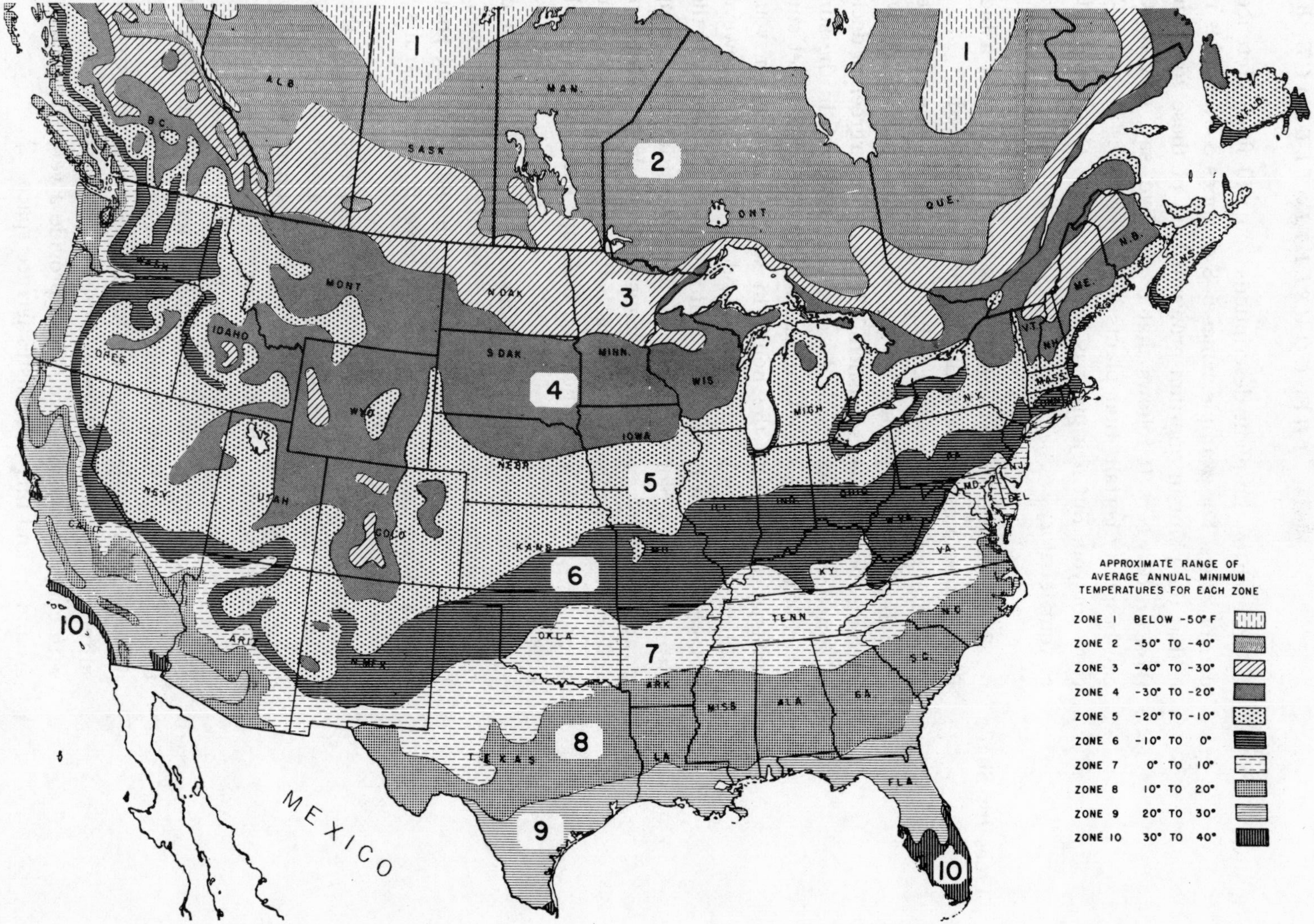

APPROXIMATE RANGE OF AVERAGE ANNUAL MINIMUM TEMPERATURES FOR EACH ZONE
ZONE 1 BELOW -50° F
ZONE 2 -50° TO -40°
ZONE 3 -40° TO -30°
ZONE 4 -30° TO -20°
ZONE 5 -20° TO -10°
ZONE 6 -10° TO 0°
ZONE 7 0° TO 10°
ZONE 8 10° TO 20°
ZONE 9 20° TO 30°
ZONE 10 30° TO 40°
1
2
3
4
5
6
7
8
9
10
MEXICO
ALB.
B.C.
SASK.
MAN.
ONT.
QUE.
N.B.
N.S.
WASH.
OREG.
CALIF.
NEV.
IDAHO
MONT.
WYO.
UTAH
ARIZ.
COLO.
N.MEX.
N.DAK.
S.DAK.
NEBR.
KANS.
OKLA.
TEXAS
MINN.
IOWA
MO.
ARK.
LA.
WIS.
ILL.
MISS.
MICH.
IND.
KY.
TENN.
ALA.
OHIO
GA.
FLA.
W.VA.
VA.
N.C.
S.C.
PA.
N.Y.
MD.
DEL.
N.J.
VT.
N.H.
ME.
MASS.
CONN.

[1] Developed by the Agricultural Research Service of the U.S. Department of Agriculture.

In each of the plant descriptions you will find reference to a pair of zones. For example, zones 5–8 or zones 3–7. All this means is that the plant in question grows in both of these zones and all those in between. It follows that if you live, say, in zone 6, you can be pretty certain that plants listed for zones 5–8 or 3–7 will grow for you. But if a plant is listed for, say, zones 8–10, it's out of your territory.

Trees for Shade   For shade on the terrace there is nothing to equal a big tree. But the tree must be carefully selected and planted.

The ideal tree for terrace shade has branches which are high enough above the ground so you can walk underneath without ducking and don't feel squashed. Whether it's evergreen or deciduous is immaterial because both do a good shading job in the summer; the choice depends therefore on whether you want to let sun onto the terrace and into the house in winter or whether you need shading and screening the year round. In either case, however, the foliage should not be so dense that it completely shuts off the sun. Sitting under a Norway maple or horse chestnut, for example, is a rather gloomy experience because the shade is dense and unbroken. A sugar maple or birch is better because beams of sunlight reach the ground, and when you look up, you can see patches of blue sky.

The ideal shade tree should also be a "clean" tree: it doesn't constantly litter the terrace and surrounding area with leaves, twigs, fruits and nuts. By the same token, it should be strong enough to withstand storms. And it shouldn't have flowers or fruits which attract an objectionable number of bees.

All trees must be planted carefully to ensure that they will make strong growth; but since this isn't a garden book, I won't get into the detailed mechanics of the business here. But I do want to emphasize the importance of planting trees so that water and oxygen can get to the roots. This means that if you plant a tree in the center of a terrace (or if you build a terrace around an existing tree), the terrace floor should be laid in sand. Then, even though the paving is carried close up to the tree trunk, the tree will not suffer for lack of moisture or oxygen. But if you surround a tree with concrete masonry, you must provide a very large open pocket around it; and this just wastes terrace space.

184

A large fenced Natchez terrace photographed in winter is built around a live oak which is itself surrounded by gold-dust plants, podocarpus, variegated euonymus and other small plants.

Trees planted around the edges of a terrace can, as a rule, survive whether the paving is solid or not, because at least half of the root system is exposed. However, if you build a free-form terrace and set a tree into a U-shaped pocket, it may get into trouble unless the paving is laid in sand.

Regardless of the paving, one problem to be reckoned with when planting a large tree is the damage the growing roots can do by heaving and breaking the paving. Trees with roots which grow near the soil surface do this more than those with deep roots. But since it's difficult to predict what any tree will do, the best precaution is to place the trunk at least 2 ft.—and preferably more—from solid paving.

If a deck is built around a tree, the hole for the trunk must be made large enough to allow for an increase in the trunk's growth and also to protect the deck against battering when wind sways the tree.

SELECTED TERRACE SHADE TREES

APPLE *Malus pumila*. Zones 3–8. Deciduous. Standard trees grow to 25–50 ft., depending on variety. An old apple can be a very picturesque tree, but needs to be pruned every couple of years to remove suckers and small branches which clutter the crown. On a terrace, fruits can be a problem since they can fall on your head, rot on the ground if you don't pick them up, and attract bees. However, most varieties do not bear fruit unless another apple tree is growing nearby. Or you can prevent fruiting by spraying in the spring with naphthalene-acetic acid.

Apples also make beautiful espaliers.

ASH, GREEN *Fraxinus pennsylvanica lanceolata*. Zones 2–7. Deciduous. 60 ft. Not the world's finest tree, but good enough. And it grows very rapidly.

BEECH, AMERICAN *Fagus grandifolia*. Warmest parts of zones 3–9. 90 ft. This is one of our most beautiful native trees with massive trunk and branches covered with beautiful light-gray bark. Leaves turn bronze in the fall and hang on a long time. The tree grows rather slowly but needs lots of space to spread. For use near a terrace, you may have to cut out the lowest branches to get enough headroom.

BEECH, EUROPEAN *Fagus sylvatica*. Zones 5–10. Deciduous. 90 ft. This is another extremely handsome, wide-spreading tree similar to the foregoing. The copper beech, with copper-colored leaves, is a favorite. And there are excellent varieties with deeply cut, fernlike leaves. Just make sure the variety you buy does not have weeping branches. Even with nonweeping types you will probably have to cut out some of the lowest branches.

BIRCH, WHITE   Also called paper birch and canoe birch. *Betula papyrifera*. Zones 2–7. Deciduous. 90 ft. An upright, not-too-wide-spreading tree that is notable for its glistening white bark and heart-shaped leaves that dance in the breeze. Plant so the gorgeous trunk is fully exposed.

When buying a white birch, beware that you are not sold a gray birch. It also has white bark, but with many more black marks; and as sold in nurseries, it usually has several trunks. You'll like its looks, but when there's a heavy snow it bends to the ground and may never stand straight again.

BLACK SALLY   *Eucalyptus stellulata*. Zones 9–10. Broadleaf evergreen. 40 ft. A wide, pendulous tree with beautiful gray bark which turns olive green. You may have to cut out the lowest branches if planted close to the terrace. With the branches left on, it forms a good screen.

CORK TREE, AMUR.   *Phellodendron amurense*. Warmest parts of zones 3–10. Deciduous. 40 ft. Though not a very large tree, the cork tree seems massive because the trunk and main limbs are huge and covered with very rough corklike bark. It is particularly handsome in winter, but good for shading the terrace in summer because of its rather open foliage.

ELM, CHINESE   *Ulmus parvifolia*. Zones 6–10. Deciduous. 60 ft. The greatest of all elms and one of the greatest of all shade trees is the American elm; but until someone figures out a surefire way of preventing Dutch elm disease, it would be folly to plant it. The Chinese elm is less beautiful but still decorative, and it grows with amazing speed. One variety which is especially popular in Southern California is known as the evergreen elm, but it is not a good terrace tree because the weeping branches often sweep the ground.

GINKGO   *Ginkgo biloba*. Zones 5–10. Deciduous. 120 ft. The ginkgo is a wide, irregular, very picturesque tree which withstands miserable growing conditions (it's a favorite for use in cities). The leaves are fan-shaped and turn yellow in the fall. The tree's only drawback is its foul-smelling fruit, but this won't bother you if you plant male trees only.

GUM, RED-SPOTTED   *Eucalyptus maculosa*. Zones 9–10. Broad-

A magnificent Atlanta terrace is made the more so by excellent planting. Apple trees are espaliered against a blank wall. Boxwood frames the large window.

leaf evergreen. 50 ft. Slender tree with drooping branches. Its lovely gray and brown bark may be something of a nuisance because it flakes off in summer, leaving a white powdery surface which rubs off on clothing. But don't let this stop you from planting it.

HEMLOCK, CANADA *Tsuga canadensis.* Zones 3–7. Needled evergreen. 90 ft. This is one of the prettiest conifers. The branches are slightly drooping, the needles short and blunt; it is bright green above and blue-green below. The effect is feathery. The tree often has several trunks, but the best specimens have one.

When young, the Canada hemlock is not a suitable terrace shade tree because the branches grow close to the ground; but with age, these are shaded out or can be cut out, and you wind up with as nice a shade tree as you could ask for. Another use for hemlocks is in tall, very dense hedges.

HEMLOCK, CAROLINA *Tsuga caroliniana.* Zones 5–8. Needled evergreen. 75 ft. To all intents and purposes, this is a dead ringer for the better-known Canada hemlock, but grows a little farther south.

HONEY LOCUST, MORAINE *Gleditsia triacanthos inermis Moraine.* Zones 5–8. Deciduous. 130 ft. The moraine honey locust is a form of thornless honey locust and one of the best shade trees because it has compound leaves with innumerable little leaflets that flutter in the breeze and let in a goodly amount of light and sun while providing ample shade. The tree is wide-spreading, flat-topped and free of troubles and does very well in cities.

IRONWOOD Also called American hornbeam and blue beech. *Carpinus caroliniana.* Zones 2–9. Deciduous. 35 ft. If you have a shady garden, the ironwood is a good choice because its natural habitat is the forest, where it grows in the shade of much larger trees. It has blue-gray bark, leaves which turn orange-red or crimson in the autumn and zigzag branches. But its prize feature is the trunk and main branches. They resemble a well-sinewed, muscular human arm.

JACARANDA *Jacaranda acutifolia.* Zone 10. Deciduous. 50 ft. This is another tree with the light, fernlike foliage which casts such excellent shade. But you will like it especially for its large clusters of violet-blue flowers in spring and summer.

MAPLE, DAVID *Acer davidii.* Zones 7–10. Deciduous. 40 ft. The David maple has big leaves which start out red, turn a glistening green and end up yellow and purple. The bark is green with white stripes.

MAPLE, SUGAR   *Acer saccharum*. Warmest parts of zones 3–10. 120 ft. The sugar maple is best known for its fiery-red fall coloring. But you will like it on all other counts, especially as it grows old and craggy. And if you want to make maple syrup, you can.

OAK, BUR   Also called mossycup oak. *Quercus macrocarpa*. Zones 4–10. Deciduous.

First a word about oaks in general. There are no more handsome trees, and no better shade trees if you have space for them. They are strong, durable and open enough to give a nice mixture of sun and shade on the terrace. But they have two faults: (1) In the fall they drop acorns all over the place; and even a tiny acorn falling from a great height can make your skull smart. (2) Oaks are the first target of the caterpillars of gypsy moths and many other pests. These not only can defoliate trees in jig time, but they also make life on a terrace miserable because they drop down out of the trees on long sticky threads. However, the pests can be controlled by spraying in the spring just as they start emerging from their nests.

The bur oak is a rugged tree with upreaching branches. It grows especially well in the Mississippi River Valley.

OAK, CANYON LIVE   *Quercus chrysolepis*. Zones 8–10. Broadleaf evergreen. 60 ft. A large rounded or spreading tree native to California.

OAK, COAST LIVE   *Quercus agrifolia*. Broadleaf evergreen. Zones 8–10. 70 ft. Another California beauty.

OAK, LIVE   *Quercus virginiana*. Zones 8–10. Broadleaf evergreen. 60 ft. The great oak of the Deep South. When fully grown, you could tuck an entire average-size suburban lot underneath.

OAK, RED   *Quercus rubra*. Zones 4–10. Deciduous. 75 ft. Upright tree with branches borne well above the ground. Beautiful fall coloring.

OAK, VALLEY   Also called California white oak. *Quercus lobata*. Zones 7–10. Deciduous. 80 ft. A massive, spreading tree. California's equivalent of the white oak.

OAK, WHITE   *Quercus alba*. Zones 5–10. Deciduous. 90 ft. The greatest of the oaks. Given space, its mighty limbs spread so far to the side that they often have to be guyed one to the other to keep them from breaking under ice.

OAK, WILLOW   *Quercus phellos*. Zones 6–9. Deciduous. 50 ft. This is the most delicate-looking oak. Its leaves resemble those of the willow.

PECAN *Carya illinoiensis*. Zones 6–9. Deciduous. 150 ft. The falling nuts can be a menace as well as a sweeping problem in the fall. Otherwise, this is a good shade tree. Allowed to grow naturally, it looks craggy and informal. But if you start pruning early, it can be given a handsome vase shape.

PINE, AUSTRIAN *Pinus nigra*. Zones 4–7. Needled evergreen. 90 ft. A very handsome tree with long stiff dark-green needles which glisten in the sun.

As young trees, all pines put out branches so close to the ground that they have no value as shade trees. But most of them grow rapidly; and as they do, the lower branches die out or can be cut off, and the trees become excellent shade makers—tall, not terribly wide, yielding a nicely sun-dappled shade which swirls with the breezes.

PINE, EASTERN WHITE *Pinus strobus*. Zones 3–6. Needled evergreen. 150 ft. The best of the pines, and one of the very best of all trees. It starts out very symmetrical; then as it grows older, it becomes tall and irregular. The needles are slender, soft green in color, and give off a delicious fragrance when they fall.

PINE, ITALIAN STONE *Pinus pinea*. Zones 9–10. Needled evergreen. 80 ft. A picturesque shade tree when fully grown. Its crown forms a great wide flat umbrella.

PINE, SCOTCH *Pinus sylvestris*. Zones 2–8. Needled evergreen. 75 ft. The needles are stiff and blue-green; and young trees are rather stiffly pyramidal and not overly pretty. But with age, the Scotch pine becomes loose and open and the branches twist around in the most surprisingly delightful ways.

PINE, WESTERN WHITE *Pinus monticola*. Zones 6–8. Needled evergreen. 90 ft. An almost exact duplicate of the Eastern white pine.

POINCIANA, ROYAL Also called Flamboyant. *Delonix regia*. Zone 10. Deciduous. 40 ft. When covered with its 3-in. scarlet and yellow flowers in spring and summer, there is no gaudier tree. You'll love it. And you will love it also in other seasons as a shade tree, because it has a wide crown and is covered with lacy foliage. An extremely fast grower.

SWEET GUM *Liquidambar styraciflua*. Zones 6–10. Deciduous. 120 ft. The sweet gum forms a fairly compact pyramid with a long, clean trunk. The star-shaped leaves are shiny green in summer, brilliant scarlet in fall.

TULIP TREE   Also called yellow poplar. *Liriodendron tulipifera.* Zones 5–10. Deciduous. 175 ft. This is the tallest-growing deciduous tree native to the United States, but don't worry about its growing beyond your property during your lifetime. It's an excellent tall, pyramidal tree with unusual, lovely leaves. In late spring it bears pretty tulip-shaped yellow-green flowers.

YATE   *Eucalyptus cornuta.* Zones 9–10. Broadleaf evergreen. 60 ft. This attractive spreading tree is not very particular about soil, water or climate conditions. It has clusters of greenish-yellow flowers in summer followed by clusters of seed capsules. Shiny leaves. Bark peels off in strips.

YELLOWWOOD   *Cladrastis lutea.* Warmest parts of zones 3–10. Deciduous. 50 ft. This is a very shapely, good-looking tree in all seasons. In late spring it has fragrant white flowers hanging in wisterialike clusters, but unfortunately these do not appear every year. The fall coloring is orange to yellow.

SELECTED SMALL TREES FOR ORNAMENT

In a pinch, some of these trees might serve as shade trees for the terrace, but their main value is for planting around the edges of the terrace and in the garden beyond to give color, form or texture. Some are slender and upright and make excellent accent plants. A few can be espaliered.

ARBORVITAE, AMERICAN   *Thuja occidentalis.* Zones 6–10 but can be grown up to zone 2 if you don't mind the brown foliage in winter. Evergreen. 60 ft. Around the terrace, the arborvitae is best kept pruned to form a not-too-tall, slender needle. Grows in shade as well as sun.

CHERRY, FLOWERING   *Prunus* species. Zones 4–10. Deciduous. 25 ft., though some varieties grow much taller. Prized for their beautiful white or pink spring flowers and glistening deep-reddish bark. The weeping Higan cherry is especially graceful, but the double-flowered Kwanzan cherry has the most spectacular bloom.

CRABAPPLE   *Malus* species. Zones 2–10. Deciduous. 25 ft., but some are taller. The crabs are even more spectacular in bloom in the spring than the flowering cherries. Some also have pretty fruits in summer and fall. There are untold numbers of varieties to choose from.

CRAPE MYRTLE   *Lagerstroemia indica.* Warmest parts of zones

7–10. Deciduous. 25 ft. The crape myrtle is especially lovely planted in front of a wall or mass of evergreens because it has a cluster of angular trunks covered with light-brown bark which flakes off. In summer the entire tree is covered with pink or red flowers.

DOGWOOD, FLOWERING *Cornus florida.* Zones 5–9. Deciduous. 40 ft. When full-size the flowering dogwood makes a good small shade tree, but it doesn't get this tall very often. In the spring it is famed for its brilliant white or pink flowers, and in fall it is covered with red berries which attract birds and squirrels. It also has deep-red autumn foliage.

DOGWOOD, JAPANESE Also called Korean dogwood. *Cornus kousa.* Deciduous. Zones 6–10. 20 ft. Though not well known, this dogwood is a worthy companion of the flowering dogwood. Use both. The Japanese tree is a little more upright and dense. The flowers—always white—have more sharply pointed petals and appear three weeks later. The fall fruits are like plump strawberries.

FALSE CYPRESS, SAWARA *Chamaecyparis pisifera.* Warmest parts of zones 3–8. Needled evergreen. 120 ft., but you can keep it much lower by pruning. It also makes an excellent tall, dense hedge. The tree is feathery-looking and lovely the year round.

FIG, WEEPING *Ficus benjamina.* Zone 10. Broadleaf evergreen. 30 ft. A very ornamental, compact tree with pendant branches and shiny leaves. Red fruits in summer. Can be espaliered. Grows in shade as well as sun.

FRANKLINIA *Franklinia alatamaha.* Zones 6–10. Deciduous. 30 ft. The franklinia is unusual among trees because it bears its lovely white-and-yellow 3-in. flowers in late summer and fall. Sometimes the flowers are in bloom after the leaves have turned scarlet. Does best in sun but will grow in light shade.

FRINGETREE *Chionanthus virginicus.* Zones 5–9. Deciduous. 30 ft. A relative of the lilacs, the fringetree has great plumes of fragrant white flowers in late spring. These are followed in the fall by blue-black fruits. Considered one of the most beautiful small trees native to the U.S.

GOLDEN-CHAIN TREE *Laburnum watereri.* Zones 6–10. Deciduous. 30 ft. A rather slender, upright tree covered in the spring with long, pendulous clusters of bright yellow flowers.

GOLDEN-RAIN TREE *Koelreuteria paniculata.* Zones 6–10. Deciduous. 30 ft. By contrast with the preceding, this tree is flat-topped and wide. Yellow flowers grow in large, upright clusters in early summer.

GRAPEFRUIT *Citrus paradisi.* Zones 9–10. Broadleaf evergreen. 30 ft. A gorgeous tree with lustrous leaves, waxy white flowers and magnificent yellow fruits in winter. It grows as wide as high.

HOLLY, AMERICAN *Ilex opaca.* Zones 6–9. Broadleaf evergreen. 50 ft. Give hollies sun and protection from cold winter wind and they will do well. The dense leaves are dark green above, lighter beneath, and spiny around the edges. The clusters of red berries last from fall into winter. They appear only on female plants, and to have them you must plant a male specimen nearby.

HOLLY, ENGLISH *Ilex aquifolium.* Warmest parts of zones 6–10. Broadleaf evergreen. 70 ft. The English holly is rated the best of all, but in this country it is superlative only in the Pacific Northwest. The berries are very red; the leaves, glossy. You need both male and female plants to have fruit.

HOLLY, LUSTERLEAF *Ilex latifolia.* Warmest parts of Zones 7–10. Broadleaf evergreen. 60 ft. The lusterleaf holly has unusually large, finely toothed, glossy leaves. The red berries are big and grow in tight clusters. Plant male and female specimens. Can be grown in partial shade as well as sun.

MAGNOLIA, SAUCER *Magnolia soulangeana.* Zones 6–10. Deciduous. 25 ft. The saucer magnolia is noted for its large white or pink to purple flowers in the spring. The tree has an interesting, often handsome shape, attractive gray bark and oddly twisted pods of bright-red seeds in the fall. Its only flaw is that the fallen flowers make an awful mess on the ground for a week or so.

MAGNOLIA, SOUTHERN *Magnolia grandiflora.* Warmest parts of zones 7–10. Broadleaf evergreen. 90 ft. This is the spectacular magnolia of the Deep South. It's pyramidal and dense and has lustrous leathery leaves, and the white flowers in late spring and early summer are beautifully shaped and fragrant. Can be grown in shade. Makes a handsome espalier.

MAGNOLIA, STAR *Magnolia stellata.* Zones 6–8. Deciduous. 20 ft. In cold climates this is the first magnolia to bloom. The white flowers are many-petaled and fragrant.

MAPLE, JAPANESE *Acer palmatum.* Zones 6–10. Deciduous. 20 ft. Few small trees are as beautiful as the Japanese maple. Spreading, irregular and sometimes shaped like large mounds, they are covered with delicately chiseled leaves which may be red throughout the growing season or may start out red in the spring, turn green in the summer and then go back to red in the fall. The coloring is best in full sun, but the tree also grows well in partial shade.

MIMOSA   Also called silktree. *Albizia julibrissin*. Zones 7–10. Deciduous. 35 ft. The mimosa makes an excellent wide, low shade tree but litters the ground too badly with leaves, twigs and flowers to be used for that purpose on a terrace. But don't hesitate to plant it away from the terrace, where you can enjoy it from afar. The foliage is fernlike. Bright-pink flowers persist for several months in warm weather.

ORANGE   *Citrus sinensis*. Zones 9–10. Broadleaf evergreen. 25 ft. Most people grow oranges for the luscious fruit, but like grapefruits and other citrus trees, they are also superb ornamentals. Dwarf varieties are available.

PALM, GUADALUPE   *Erythea edulis*. Zones 9–10. 30 ft. Broadleaf evergreen. This palm has a spreading top with light-green fronds and white flowers.

PALM, MEDITERRANEAN FAN   *Chamaerops humilis*. Zones 9–10. Broadleaf evergreen. 20 ft. A very hardy palm tree which develops into a clump.

PALM, PIGMY DATE   *Phoenix roebelenii*. Zone 10. Broadleaf evergreen. 6 ft. Single-stemmed palm with a dense clump of fronds. Needs shade.

PALM, SENEGAL DATE   *Phoenix reclinata*. Zone 10. Broadleaf evergreen. 25 ft. The Senegal date palm puts up a graceful cluster of curving trunks topped with feathery fronds.

PEACH   *Prunus persica*. Zones 5–9. Deciduous. 25 ft. If you don't butcher a peach tree when you prune it to encourage fruit development, it makes a pretty specimen with deep-pink flowers in early spring and long, glossy leaves through the summer. Fruits ripen from mid-summer on, depending on the variety. How delicious they are! Unfortunately, regular spraying is necessary to assure perfect fruit, but that's a small price to pay for the rewards.

PERSIMMON, JAPANESE   *Diospyros kaki*. Warmest parts of zones 7–10. Deciduous. 40 ft. The Japanese persimmon has just about everything: a fine shape, handsome foliage which is orange or scarlet in the fall, delectable orange fruits which ripen before the leaves fall and hang on the tree long afterward.

196

A great boulder and a Japanese red pine decorate the corner of a terrace and soften the lines of the blank wall behind.

PITTOSPORUM, QUEENSLAND   *Pittosporum rhombifolium.* Zone 10. Broadleaf evergreen. 30 ft. A shapely tree with white flowers in the spring and showy orange fruits in clusters in fall and winter. The foliage is glossy. Grows in partial shade or sun.

RUSSIAN OLIVE   *Elaeagnus angustifolia.* Zones 2–9. Deciduous. 20 ft. This wide, spiny tree has slender gray-green leaves which dance and billow in the breeze and contrast delightfully with other garden plants. There are fragrant yellow and silver flowers in the spring; yellow and silver berries in fall.

SCHEFFLERA   Also called Queensland umbrella tree. *Brassaia actinophylla.* Zone 10. Broadleaf evergreen. 25 ft. Schefflera has

197

enormous compound leaves divided into large shiny leaflets which hang like the ribs of an umbrella. Exotic red flowers in summer arch above the foliage. Then come little purple fruits.

SEAGRAPE   *Coccoloba uvifera.* Zones 9–10. Broadleaf evergreen. 20 ft. The leaves of the seagrape are like large leathery, rounded fans, and when the wind blows they do a spectacular dance. The tree usually has several trunks covered with mottled bark. Seen against the sky or a white wall, it makes a handsome, bold display.

SNOWBELL, JAPANESE   *Styrax japonica.* Zones 6–10. Deciduous. 30 ft. This is a wide, flat-topped tree with horizontal branches from which fragrant white, bell-shaped flowers hang in solid rows in late spring. Sun or light shade.

STEWARTIA, JAPANESE   *Stewartia pseudo-camellia.* Zones 6–10. Deciduous. 60 ft. In early summer, the stewartia is well covered with fragrant white flowers resembling camellias. In the fall the bright-green leaves turn purplish. In the winter, you can see the handsome reddish-brown, flaking bark. All in all, an excellent tree. It can be espaliered.

TEA TREE, AUSTRALIAN   *Leptospermum laevigatum.* Zone 10. Broadleaf evergreen. 30 ft. If planted in the open, the tea tree develops a twisted trunk with an umbrellalike canopy of small leaves and white spring flowers. It brings the Orient to the garden.

THORN, WASHINGTON   *Crataegus phaenopyrum.* Zones 5–10. Deciduous. 30 ft. There are many good species of hawthorn, but this is probably the best for this country. It has white flowers in spring; bright-red berries from the fall well into the winter. The nicely chiseled leaves are a lustrous green which turns red.

UMBRELLA PINE   *Sciadopitys verticillata.* Zones 6–10. Needled evergreen. 50 ft. The umbrella pine is an extremely slow-growing tree forming a dense pyramid. The needles are long and deep, deep green. They radiate out from the twigs like the ribs of an umbrella.

YEW, HICKS   *Taxus media hicksii.* Zones 3–10. Needled evergreen. 20 ft. By regular pruning you can shape this tree into a small, slender column which serves as an outstanding accent plant. It forms a wide vase otherwise. The needles are short and dark green. All parts of the yews are poisonous if eaten.

YEW, IRISH   *Taxus baccata stricta.* Zones 7–10. Needled evergreen. 25 ft. This looks like a well-pruned Hicks yew grown very large. It's an imposing, formal, dark-green pillar.

Shrubs   Although it's possible that you may want a few large shrubs on or next to the terrace, the chances are that you will rely on shrubs which are naturally small or can be kept small by pruning. There are a great many to choose from. Since their root systems are comparatively small, all can be planted in the middle of a solid-masonry terrace, but you should make each plant pocket at least 2 ft. across.

Note that some favorite shrubs require acid soil. To determine the condition of your soil, send a half-pint sample to your State Agricultural Extension Service for analysis. If the report you get back shows the soil has a pH of 6.5 or higher, mix well-rotted oak leaves or pine needles into it to increase acidity.

SELECTED SHRUBS FOR PLANTING ON OR CLOSE TO THE TERRACE

ABELIA, GLOSSY   *Abelia grandiflora.* Zones 6–10. Evergreen in warm climates; deciduous elsewhere. 6 ft. Graceful plant with arching branches and clusters of white to pink flowers from early summer into fall. Can take some shade.

ANDROMEDA, JAPANESE   *Pieris japonica.* Zones 6–9. Broadleaf evergreen. 9 ft. A superlative shrub. One of the earliest to bloom in the spring, it's covered with creamy-white drooping flower sprays. Young leaves are bronze-colored, then turn bright green. Sun or partial shade.

ANDROMEDA, MOUNTAIN   *Pieris floribunda.* Zones 5–9. Broadleaf evergreen. 6 ft. Like the preceding but later flowers in upright clusters.

AUCUBA, JAPANESE   *Aucuba japonica.* Warmest parts of zones 7–10. Broadleaf evergreen. 10 ft. Shade lover. Very wide-spreading. Red flowers in spring. Bright-red berries on female plants in fall (you must plant a male specimen nearby). Leaves are long and glossy. On the popular gold-dust plant, they are splattered with gold marks.

AZALEA   *Rhododendron* species. Broadleaf evergreens; also deciduous species. Zones 5–10. 3–15 ft. Azaleas are our most sensational bloomers. Among the outstanding types are the Exbury, Ghent, Indian and Mollis hybrids; and the flame, Kurume, royal, snow and torch azaleas. Use those which are most highly recommended by knowledgeable nurserymen for your area. All need acid soil. If possible, plant where they will get sun in the morning or afternoon but not at midday.

BOX, COMMON Also called boxwood. *Buxus sempervirens.* Zones 6–10. Broadleaf evergreen. 20 ft. Dense and dark-green. Too big for near terrace if you intend to let it grow, but excellent if you keep it pruned or sheared. You can also plant a dwarf variety. Sun or shade.

BOX, KOREAN *Buxus microphylla koreana.* Zones 5–8. Broadleaf evergreen. 4 ft. Very much like the preceding, but smaller and hardier.

BRIDAL WREATH *Spiraea vanhouttei.* Zones 5–9. Deciduous. 6 ft. Fast grower with arching branches and clusters of white flowers in late spring.

BROOM, WARMINSTER *Cytisus praecox.* Zones 6–10. Deciduous. 6 ft. Broom forms a mass of billowing, swirling, slender twigs which are bright green all year. The plant is completely covered with yellow flowers in spring.

CAMELLIA, COMMON *Camellia japonica.* Warmest parts of Zones 7–10. Broadleaf evergreen. 20 ft., but given time may develop into a 40-ft. tree. It can be kept much smaller. Favorite flowering plant for sunny or partially shaded areas. Single or double flowers in whites, pinks, reds and variegated colors. They bloom from fall into late winter. Needs slightly acid soil.

CAMELLIA, SASANQUA *Camellia sasanqua.* Warmest parts of Zones 7–10. Broadleaf evergreen. 20 ft. The flowers are smaller than the common camellias, but they appear several weeks earlier.

CAROLINA ALLSPICE Also called sweetshrub. *Calycanthus floridus.* Zones 5–10. Deciduous. 9 ft. Plant in sun or partial shade for its aromatic foliage and fragrant red-brown spring flowers.

CINQUEFOIL, SHRUBBY *Potentilla fruticosa.* Zones 3–10. Deciduous. 4 ft. Feathery-leaved plant covered with yellow flowers for most of the summer. Good for edgings and low hedges.

COTONEASTER, ROCKSPRAY *Cotoneaster horizontalis.* Zones 5–10. Deciduous. 3 ft. This is a low, wide-spreading plant with countless little red berries in the fall. Excellent for planting along the upper edges of raised terraces so the branches can droop down over the edges.

DEUTZIA, SLENDER *Deutzia gracilis.* Zones 5–9. Deciduous. 3 ft. Almost smothered by white flowers in spring. Sun or partial shade.

ENKIANTHUS, REDVEIN *Enkianthus campanulatus.* Zones 5–10. Deciduous. 20 ft. An excellent shrub which can be kept tall and compact by pruning. Clusters of orange, lily-of-the-valley-like flowers in spring. Brilliant red foliage in fall. Can take some shade.

FATSHEDERA *Fatshedera lizei.* Warmest parts of zones 7–10. Broadleaf evergreen. 7 ft. Needs shade. Large, handsome, pointed leaves. Shrub must be staked to keep it growing upright.

FATSIA *Fatsia japonica.* Warmest parts of zones 7–10. Broadleaf evergreen. 8 ft. You have never seen such handsome leaves. They're up to 15 in. across, glossy, dark green, shaped like stars. Plant in shade.

FIRETHORN, LALAND'S SCARLET *Pyracantha coccinea lalandei.* Warmest parts of zones 6–10. Evergreen in warm climates; deciduous elsewhere. 10 ft. This is a very thorny plant, but if you want a sensational espalier, it's among the best. Whitish flowers in spring are followed by great clusters of orange-red berries in fall. Sun or partial shade.

A firethorn espalier in the making. When completed, all the branches will reach out horizontally and then turn down.

FIRETHORN, FORMOSA *Pyracantha koidzumii.* Zones 8–10. Evergreen. 10 ft. Like the foregoing, except that it has brilliant red berries. The outstanding firethorn for warm climates.

FOTHERGILLA, DWARF *Fothergilla gardenii.* Zones 6–9. Deciduous. 3 ft. Spring flowers form interesting little white tufts. Handsome leaves turn yellow, orange and red in fall. Plant in partial shade.

FUCHSIA *Fuchsia* species. Warmest parts of zones 7–10. Deciduous or evergreen. Up to 12 ft. Very variable plants but all with charming, drooping flowers in whites, reds, blues or purples. Need filtered sun and protection from wind.

HEAVENLY BAMBOO *Nandina domestica.* Zones 8–10. Broadleaf evergreen. 8 ft. An outstandingly graceful plant for silhouetting against a wall. It has many slender canes tipped with lacy foliage that moves in a breeze. Big clusters of white flowers in early summer. Bright-red berries in fall.

HIBISCUS, CHINESE *Hibiscus rosa-sinensis.* Zones 9–10. Broadleaf evergreen. 15 ft., but use smaller varieties near the terrace. One of our great flowering shrubs, hibiscus has enormous blossoms in many shades of white, pink, red, yellow and orange. Prefers sun but withstands light shade. Slightly acid soil.

HOLLY, CHINESE *Ilex cornuta.* Warmest parts of zones 7–10. Broadleaf evergreen. 10 ft. Exceptionally beautiful holly with brilliant big red berries in fall and winter, and large waxy leaves. Slightly acid soil.

HOLLY, CONVEX JAPANESE *Ilex crenata convexa.* Zones 6–10. Broadleaf evergreen. 9 ft. You could easily mistake this indispensable holly for boxwood. It has leaves of the same shape and size but shinier. The berries are black. Plant can be pruned to almost any size and shape. Sun or partial shade.

HOLLY, HELLER'S *Ilex crenata helleri.* Zones 6–10. Broadleaf evergreen. 4 ft. Can be held to only 1 ft. in height. A perfect plant for edgings and low hedges and as specimen plants in the front of shrubbery borders.

HYDRANGEA, OAKLEAF *Hydrangea quercifolia.* Zones 6–10. Deciduous. 6 ft. Though much less gaudy than the garden hydrangea with its blue-and-pink flowers, this is a superior shrub. White flowers in clusters in early summer. Oak-leaf-shaped leaves turn bronze-red in fall. Sun or partial shade.

HYPERICUM, HIDCOTE *Hypericum patulum Hidcote.* Warmest parts of zones 6–10. Evergreen in warm climates; deciduous elsewhere. 3 ft. Use hypericum for color throughout the summer. Flowers are bright yellow and fragrant.

JUNIPER, MEYER *Juniperus squamata meyeri.* Zones 5–10. Needled evergreen. 12 ft. but for use on a terrace, it should be kept smaller. The plant is upright and bluish green.

JUNIPER, PFITZER *Juniperus chinensis pfitzeriana.* Zones 5–10. Needled evergreen. 10 ft. Best-known of the shrubby junipers, this one spreads outward and upward but takes kindly to hard pruning. Bright-blue berries in fall and winter on female plants.

LAVENDER *Lavandula officinalis.* Zones 6–10. Broadleaf evergreen. 3 ft. Plant the little, gray-leaved lavender for its old-fashioned, fragrant flowers.

LEUCOTHOE, DROOPING *Leucothoe fontanesiana.* Zones 5–9. Broadleaf evergreen. 6 ft. Low, spreading shrub for a partially shaded bed with acid soil. Graceful foliage turns bronzy in fall. Bell-shaped white flowers hang in clusters from arching branches in late spring.

LILAC, KOREAN *Syringa palibiniana.* Zones 5–8. Deciduous. 3 ft. Fragrant lilac flowers in midspring. The smallest of the lilacs.

LILAC, PERSIAN *Syringa persica.* Zones 6–8. Deciduous. 6 ft. Compact, upright shrub with delightfully fragrant pale-lilac flowers.

LILAC, SWEGIFLEXA *Syringa swegiflexa.* Zones 6–8. Deciduous. 9 ft., but can be kept smaller. Lovely fragrant pink flowers.

MAHONIA, LEATHERLEAF *Mahonia bealei.* Zones 7–10. Broadleaf evergreen. 10 ft. Handsome spiny, gray-green leaves; clusters of yellow spring flowers; blue berries in summer. A striking plant for light shade. Prune to keep smaller.

MANZANITA, STANFORD *Arctostaphylos stanfordiana.* Warmest parts of zones 7–10. Broadleaf evergreen. 6 ft. A California plant with glossy foliage and pink flower clusters in late winter and early spring.

OREGON GRAPE *Mahonia aquifolium.* Zones 6–10. Broadleaf evergreen. 6 ft. A startling plant in winter because the hollylike leaves turn rich purple. Bright-yellow flowers in early spring are succeeded by blue grapelike fruits in summer. Partial shade or sun.

PEONY, TREE *Paeonia suffruticosa.* Zones 6–10. Deciduous. 5 ft. If you think ordinary garden peonies are beautiful, you should see these enormous spring flowers. Prefers partial shade.

PINE, MUGO *Pinus mugo mughus.* Zones 2–9. Needled evergreen. Up to 8 ft., but usually much smaller and sometimes almost prostrate. This is a true pine tree, but it forms a large low dark-green mound. Excellent for shrubbery borders and for planting at the top of a low terrace wall.

RHODODENDRON   *Rhododendron* species. Zones 5–10. Broadleaf evergreens. 6–15 ft. When a well-grown rhododendron is covered with bloom in the spring, it's something to behold. At other times, the dark-green foliage forms a fine background for smaller plants. Ask a local nurseryman which species do well in your area. Among the best are the Carolina and Korean rhododendrons and the catawba hybrids. All need a mixture of shade and sun; acid soil.

SARCOCOCCA, DWARF   *Sarcococca hookeriana humilis.* Zones 7–10. Broadleaf evergreen. 3 ft. This is a tidy, lustrous foliage plant for partial to deep shade.

SKIMMIA, REEVES   *Skimmia reevesiana.* Warmest parts of zones 7–9. Broadleaf evergreen. 2 ft. Skimmia forms a neat, attractive mound with fragrant white flowers in spring and dull-red berries in fall. Partial shade.

VIBURNUM, BURKWOOD   *Viburnum burkwoodii.* Zones 6–10. Deciduous. 6 ft. Viburnums are highly esteemed for their spring flowers, fall berries and shapely forms. Burkwood viburnum has very fragrant flowers turning from pale pink to white, and black berries. It can be espaliered. Sun or partial shade.

VIBURNUM, KOREAN SPICE   *Viburnum carlesii.* Zones 5–10. Deciduous. 5 ft. Very fragrant white flowers. Blue-black berries.

YEW, JAPANESE   *Taxus cuspidata densa.* Zones 5–10. Needled evergreen. 4 ft. This is among the smallest of the wide-spreading Japanese yews. It is extremely useful in shrubbery borders and hedges. Red berries on female plants. All parts are poisonous if eaten. Sun or light shade.

YEW, SPREADING ENGLISH   *Taxus baccata repandens.* Warmest parts of zones 6–10. Needled evergreen. 3 ft. A low spreading dark-green plant with pendulous branchlets. Red berries on female plants. Sun or shade.

LARGE SHRUBS FOR SCREENS AND HEDGES

CHERRY, NANKING   *Prunus tomentosa.* Zones 2–10. Deciduous. 9 ft. Spreading, rounded plant with many stems. Covered in early spring with white or pink flowers; then come edible red cherries.

COTONEASTER, SPREADING   *Cotoneaster divaricata.* Zones 6–10. Deciduous. 6 ft. Stiff, arching branches covered with pink flowers in spring and red berries in fall.

COTONEASTER, WILLOWLEAF *Cotoneaster salicifolia.* Warmest parts of zones 6–10. Evergreen in warm climates; deciduous elsewhere. 15 ft. Arching branches with willowlike leaves, white flowers and red berries.

ELAEAGNUS, THORNY *Elaeagnus pungens.* Warmest parts of zones 7–10. Broadleaf evergreen. 12 ft. When the wind blows, the thorny elaeagnus shows the undersides of its leaves and the whole plant glistens like silver. Fragrant yellow-white spring flowers. Silver-and-brown berries in fall. Plant needs to be pruned to prevent sprawling. Can be used in a hedge as low as 4 ft.

EUONYMUS, EVERGREEN *Euonymus japonicus.* Zones 8–9. Broadleaf evergreen. 15 ft. Glossy-leaved plant with small pink-and-orange autumn fruits. Some varieties have variegated foliage. Sun or shade.

EUONYMUS, WINGED *Euonymus alatus.* Warmest parts of zones 3–8. Deciduous. 10 ft. An outstanding shrub with very dense irregular branches covered with corky wings. Leaves turn a lovely soft red in the fall. Sun or partial shade.

FORSYTHIA, BORDER *Forsythia intermedia.* Zones 6–8. Deciduous. 9 ft. Forsythia is prized for the brilliant yellow show it makes in the spring. In other seasons, it is simply green and dense. A rapid grower.

HAWTHORN, YEDDO *Raphiolepis umbellata.* Warmest parts of zones 7–10. Broadleaf evergreen. 10 ft. Excellent as an informal screen or formal hedge as low as 4 ft. Leathery, glossy, black-green leaves. Clusters of fragrant white flowers in late spring. Blue-black berries in fall and winter.

HONEYSUCKLE, TATARIAN *Lonicera tatarica.* Warmest parts of zones 3–10. Deciduous. 9 ft. A dense, fast-growing shrub with white, pink or red flowers in late spring and red berries in summer. Sun or partial shade.

HONEYSUCKLE, WINTER *Lonicera fragrantissima.* Zones 6–10. Evergreen in warm climates; deciduous elsewhere. 6 ft. Very fragrant, white flowers in early spring followed by red berries in late spring.

LAUREL, MOUNTAIN *Kalmia latifolia.* Zones 5–8. Broadleaf evergreen. 30 ft. Mountain laurel ranks right up at the top in excellence. Its green leaves are always beautiful even in zero weather. The big clusters of delicately shaped white, pink or almost red spring flowers are simply superb. Sun or partial shade.

LILAC, COMMON *Syringa vulgaris.* Warmest parts of zones 3–

205

8. Deciduous. 20 ft. Lilacs have been an American favorite since early pioneer days. The plants are upright and many-stemmed, and in midspring they are blanketed with pretty upright clusters of fragrant purple, lilac, blue, white, pink or red flowers.

LILAC, LITTLELEAF   Also called Daphne lilac. *Syringa microphylla superba*. Zones 6–8. Deciduous. 6 ft. Grows almost twice as wide as high. Blanketed in midspring with fragrant, deep-pink flower clusters which sometimes reappear in the fall.

MYRTLE, TRUE   *Myrtus communis*. Zones 8–10. Broadleaf evergreen. 15 ft. A dense, round shrub with glossy leaves which give off a pleasant aroma when crushed. Makes a good clipped hedge; also used as an informal screen. Sun or partial shade.

NATAL PLUM   *Carissa grandiflora*. Zones 9–10. Broadleaf evergreen. 15 ft. If you want to prevent people not only from looking into but also from entering your property, plant natal plum. It has wicked spines. It also has dense, glossy foliage; jasmine-scented, white flowers more or less the year round; and edible red fruits.

OLEANDER   *Nerium oleander*. Zones 8–10. Broadleaf evergreen. 20 ft. This is a top-notch shrub for screening as well as for ornament. It's covered from spring to fall with large white, pink, red or yellow flowers. All parts of the plant are poisonous if eaten.

OSMANTHUS, HOLLY   *Osmanthus heterophyllus*. Warmest parts of zones 6–10. Broadleaf evergreen. 18 ft. Osmanthus resembles a dense holly but has fragrant yellowish flowers in early summer and blue-black berries in the fall.

PITTOSPORUM, JAPANESE   *Pittosporum tobira*. Zones 8–10. Broadleaf evergreen. 15 ft. Dense, leathery leaves in rosettes. Fragrant, creamy-white flowers in early spring. Green or brown fruits in fall open to reveal orange seeds. Needs sun or partial shade.

PRIVET, CALIFORNIA   *Ligustrum ovalifolium*. Zones 6–10. Evergreen in warm climates; deciduous elsewhere. 15 ft. The most popular hedge plant in the United States. It grows rapidly but can be kept sheared to almost any height. The leaves are a glossy dark green. Creamy-white flower clusters in early summer fill the air with fragrance. Grows in sun or partial shade.

PRIVET, JAPANESE   *Ligustrum japonicum*. Warmest parts of zones 7–10. Broadleaf evergreen. 12 ft. Like the foregoing but even handsomer.

TALLHEDGE   *Rhamnus frangula columnaris*. Zones 2–8. Deciduous. 15 ft. Tallhedge is a new hedge plant which grows rapidly upward but rarely spreads more than 4 ft. The foliage is green and glossy, and turns yellow in the fall. Red berries in late summer.

VIBURNUM, DOUBLEFILE *Viburnum plicatum tomentosum.* Zones 5–10. Deciduous. 9 ft. One of the very best viburnums. The numerous horizontal branches are covered from end to end with unusual lovely white flowers in midspring. Then in the fall come flat, thick clusters of red berries. Sun or partial shade.

VIBURNUM, SIEBOLD *Viburnum sieboldii.* Zones 5–9. Deciduous. 10 ft. White flowers in large flat clusters in late spring followed by red berries in midsummer. The foliage turns red in the fall.

VIBURNUM, TEA *Viburnum seterigum.* Zones 6–10. Deciduous. 12 ft. The red or orange berries of the tea viburnum are unequaled. They are borne in large, pendulous clusters in the fall. White flowers in early summer.

Shrubs for Hedges and Edgings Under 2 Ft. Tall

	Minimum trimmed height (ft.)	Space between plants (ft.)	Deciduous or evergreen	Climate zones
Barberry, box	1½	1	D	5–9
Barberry, crimson pigmy	1	1	D	5–9
Box, edging	1½	1	E	6–8
Cinquefoil, shrubby	1	1½	D	3–10
Deutzia, slender	1½	1½	D	5–9
Holly, Heller's	1½	1½	E	6–10
Hypericum, hidcote	1½	1½	E	6–10
Ninebark, dwarf Eastern	1½	1	D	2–8
Pine, mugo	2	2	E	2–9
Privet, Vicary golden	1	1	D	5–10
Sarcococca, dwarf	1½	1	E	7–10
Skimmia, Reeves	1½	1	E	7–9

Vines   Vines have three primary purposes on the terrace: (1) to provide color, texture and sometimes fragrance; (2) to provide shade; (3) to provide privacy. They are also sometimes used to conceal unattractive walls.

The main problem with vines which are used for shading or privacy is that you must construct something for them to grow on.

*Wires are stretched
across both of these terraces
so that deciduous vines
can be trained across to give
shade in summer.*

Exactly what this structure is depends on the way in which the vines grow, their weight and their size.

Large heavy vines which grow by twining or by tendrils or need to be guided by hand and tied in place require a sturdy structure made of decay-resistant wood which does not have to be painted. On the other hand, small, lightweight vines which grow by twining or by tendrils or need to be guided by hand require nothing more than a network of galvanized-steel or aluminum wires.

Vines that grow by means of holdfasts that cling to solid surfaces must be planted close to a wall only. For most vines the wall should be slightly rough, but a few can cling to a slick surface. All such vines present problems, however, because if grown on wood walls they tend to trap moisture and cause the wood to decay, and on masonry walls they often pull the mortar out of the joints. Furthermore, if you want to paint a wall or repair it, you must cut the vines to the ground because if they are pulled down they won't reattach themselves to the wall.

Despite their need for support, vines have certain advantages over trees, which are their principal competition as shaders and screeners. For one thing, they usually grow fast; consequently you can achieve the effect you're seeking within a year or two. For another thing, you have complete control over their growth and can train them to grow exactly where you want them.

SELECTED VINES FOR GROWING ON A PERGOLA TO SHADE THE TERRACE

Vines for this purpose must grow quite large and require little if any training. They should also be clean plants which are not overly attractive to bees.

ACTINIDIA, CHINESE   *Actinidia chinensis*. Zones 8–10. Deciduous. 30 ft. A vigorous, twining vine with dense foliage. Fragrant, creamy-white flowers in late spring.

AKEBIA, FIVE-LEAF   *Akebia quinata*. Zones 3–10. Deciduous. 30 ft. A very fast-growing twining vine with pretty foliage and clusters of fragrant purple flowers in spring. It may also have purple fruits.

AMPELOPSIS, PORCELAIN   *Ampelopsis brevipedunculata*. Zones 5–10. Deciduous. 20 ft. Strong, not-too-dense vine which climbs by tendrils. Autumn berry clusters have green, lilac, yellow and blue berries all at one time.

Entrance terrace is shaded by wisteria which clambers over an intricate trellis that casts considerable shade itself. Vigorous, heavy vines like wisteria require a very large, sturdy framework to grow on.

BOUGAINVILLEA   *Bougainvillea* varieties. Zone 10. Evergreen. 20 ft. A dense twining vine with exciting flowers in several colors in summer and fall.

CROSSVINE   *Bignonia capreolata.* Zones 7–10. Evergreen. 50 ft. Climbs by tendrils. Innumerable orange-red flowers in spring.

DUTCHMAN'S PIPE   *Aristolochia macrophylla.* Zones 5–10. Deciduous. 25 ft. Twining vine with dark-green foliage which almost hides the small meerschaum-pipe-shaped flowers. Should not be exposed to too much wind.

GRAPE   *Vitis* species. Zones 3–10. Deciduous. 60 ft. Grapes are rampant vines climbing by tendrils. The big leaves form a good but not-too-dense sunshade. Delicious fruits are borne in late summer and fall.

HERALD'S TRUMPET   *Beaumontia grandiflora.* Zone 10. Evergreen. 30 ft. Vine with lush foliage and fragrant white trumpet-shaped flowers in summer. It is semitwining but needs to be guided to some extent.

SILVERLACE VINE   *Polygonum aubertii.* Zones 5–10. Deciduous. 20 ft. Billowy, twining vine which can make much growth in a year. In late summer it is blanketed with small white flowers.

WISTERIA, CHINESE   *Wisteria sinensis.* Zones 6–10. Deciduous. 25 ft. Very vigorous twining vine. Big pendulous clusters of fragrant blue or white flowers in spring.

WISTERIA, JAPANESE   *Wisteria floribunda.* Zones 5–10. Deciduous. 25 ft. Like the preceding, but the flower clusters are much larger and appear also in pink and purple.

SELECTED VINES FOR GROWING ON A TRELLIS TO SERVE AS A SCREEN

All the vines in the foregoing list are suitable for this purpose. Others are as follows:

CLEMATIS   *Clematis* species and hybrids. Zones 4–8. Deciduous and evergreen. Up to 20 ft. A large family of vines climbing by means of tendrils. Flowers in many colors, some of them extremely large, some fragrant. The plants need sun but the roots should be in the shade.

HONEYSUCKLE, HALL'S   *Lonicera japonica halliana.* Zones 5–10. Semievergreen. Dense, easy-to-grow twining vine with fragrant flowers which turn from white to yellow in the spring. Black berries in fall. Sun or partial shade.

HONEYSUCKLE, HENRY'S   *Lonicera henryi.* Zones 5–10. Semievergreen. 12 ft. Twining vine with reddish flowers in late spring; black berries in fall.

JASMINE, COMMON WHITE   *Jasminum officinale*. Zones 8–10. Semievergreen. 30 ft. Easygoing vine with fragrant white flowers throughout the summer. Needs to be trained by hand.

MORNING GLORY   *Ipomoea purpurea*. Zones 2–10. 15 ft. This twining vine is an annual grown each year from seed, so it forms an effective screen only in the latter part of the summer. But the blue, white or red flowers are so showy you'll probably want to use it anyway.

JASMINE, STAR   *Trachelospermum jasminoides*. Zones 9–10. Evergreen. 20 ft. A dark-green vine with extremely fragrant white flowers in the spring. Twining, but needs some guidance. Plant in partial shade.

ROSE   *Rosa* species and varieties. Zones 4–10. Deciduous. 20 ft. The climbing, rambler and pillar roses are not true vines because they must be trained by hand; but they make beautiful vinelike screens covered in the spring with white, pink, red or yellow blossoms. Some varieties also bloom in the fall, and others bloom more or less steadily throughout the growing season.

SELECTED VINES THAT CLING TO WALLS

FIG, CREEPING   *Ficus pumila*. Zone 10. Evergreen. 50 ft. A dense vine with lovely tiny leaves when young, but as it grows older the leaves become larger and the plant loses its delicacy. So it must be cut back hard every few years.

HYDRANGEA, CLIMBING   *Hydrangea anomala petiolaris*. Zones 5–10. Deciduous. 75 ft. This is a massive vine with excellent foliage, interesting reddish bark and large clusters of white flowers in late spring. Sun or partial shade.

IVY, BOSTON   *Parthenocissus tricuspidata*. Zones 3–10. Deciduous. 60 ft. Grown primarily for its foliage, which turns scarlet in the fall.

IVY, ENGLISH   *Hedera helix*. Zones 6–10. Evergreen. 75 ft. This is the most beautiful vine for covering walls (and also the ground). There are many varieties. My favorite, called 238th Street, has unusually big, glossy leaves and is festooned throughout the winter with clusters of blue berries; but it is difficult to come by. Grow in sun or shade.

TRUMPET VINE   *Campsis radicans*. Zones 5–10. Deciduous. 25

ft. A large, heavy, informal vine with pleasant foliage and orange flowers in summer. It clings to walls by means of holdfasts but often needs to be tied as well.

VIRGINIA CREEPER *Parthenocissus quinquefolia.* Zones 3–10. Deciduous. 40 ft. Good foliage vine turning red in the autumn.

WINTERCREEPER *Euonymus fortunei.* Zones 4–9. Evergreen. 20 ft. Wintercreeper has handsome foliage which in some varieties is variegated. In the fall it is well covered with clusters of orange berries. Plant in sun or partial shade.

Ground Covers   In terrace plantings ground covers are used to fill beds in which you want something low, green and easy to maintain. Since space is usually limited, the best species for planting are those that do not run rampant.

SELECTED GROUND COVERS FOR TERRACE PLANTINGS   COTONEASTER, BEARBERRY *Cotoneaster dammeri.* Zones 5–10. Evergreen. 1 ft. Covered with red berries in fall. Sun or partial shade.

PAXISTIMA *Paxistima canbyi.* Zones 4–10. Evergreen. 1 ft. Tiny, dense, glossy leaves. Sun or shade.

PACHYSANDRA *Pachysandra terminalis.* Zones 4–10. Evergreen. 1 ft. Outstanding ground cover for shady areas but also grows in considerable sun if you keep it well watered and fertilized.

PERIWINKLE Also called myrtle. *Vinca minor.* Zones 4–10. Evergreen. 8 in. Excellent plant with dark-green, shiny foliage and charming blue flowers in the spring. Sun or shade.

WANDERING JEW *Zebrina pendula.* Zone 10. Evergreen. 6 in. Purple and white foliage. Partial shade.

Roses   In addition to climbing roses, two other types of rose may be grown on or around the terrace: shrub roses and just plain roses. The latter group, technically, is made up of hybrid tea roses, floribundas, grandifloras, etc.; but to the average person all are known simply as roses because they are the roses most often grown in gardens.

Few if any flowers are as heart-stoppingly beautiful as ordinary garden roses. And for that reason, you may be strongly tempted to grow them on the terrace. but they have one flaw which should make you hesitate: in winter, when they lose their leaves, the plants are anything but pretty. And in cold climates it is customary to increase their unprettiness by mounding soil high up around them.

I realize that this may not strike you as a very serious matter: most people don't worry about what their gardens look like in winter. But I have been on a crusade lately to change this attitude, because I believe gardens can be and should be just about as beautiful in winter as they are in summer; and the first step in making them beautiful is to remove from view of the house everything that is unattractive.

What I am saying, in other words, is that while it's a wonderful idea to plant garden roses on the terrace, they should be placed where you can't see them when you look out of the window at the terrace in winter. And that may take some doing.

Shrub roses, on the other hand, usually need not be concealed. Most—but not all—have more attractive shapes than garden roses. They are hardy enough so they don't need to be protected by soil mounds in the winter. And as a rule, they are planted in among other shrubs which help to hide them (garden roses, by contrast, are normally planted in a bed by themselves, although there is no rule requiring such treatment).

Regardless of the kinds of roses you plant, all must have at least six hours of sun per day. For best bloom, all need the equivalent of about 1 in. of rainfall a week. In addition, garden roses must be sprayed regularly to protect them against insects and diseases.

Selecting roses is very much a personal proposition. I, for instance, cannot abide lilac-colored roses and wouldn't recommend one even if it were rated the world's outstanding rose. The best way to get what you want is to collect the catalogs of the several big firms that specialize in growing roses, and study them.

Ferns

Ferns are beautiful, not because they are exquisitely colored but because of their delicate form and texture. Whether planted in clumps among shrubs or given an entire bed to themselves, they bring a quiet charm to terrace and garden. What's more, they require no attention.

There are many species. Most come up early in the spring and die down in the fall, but some are evergreen. A few grow in the sun, but the majority prefer shade, which makes them ideal for planting along the north side of a terrace and in other shady areas

To break up this large terrace, landscape architect Gertrude Kuh put easily maintained planting beds in the corners, around the edges and right in the middle.

which are safe from traffic. (Ferns are easily broken and crushed.)

Unfortunately, not many plant dealers sell ferns (except of the greenhouse variety), so the best way to collect them is to dig them up along the highway or wherever you find a friendly property owner who has more than he needs.

Cacti and Succulents

Grown mainly in the southwest, these are fascinating plants and sometimes very pretty. But they are difficult to use attractively in the garden except in containers. Those with spines are also dangerous.

Flowers

Under this heading come annuals, perennials, biennials and bulbs. What a vast array of beauty they offer! Yet surprisingly, flowers are not grown on many terraces except in containers. If there's any reason for this other than laziness on the part of home-owners, I suppose it is that the great majority of flowers bloom for only part of the long period the terrace is in use; and most people don't want to devote space to plants which die down and leave a hole or which must be replaced.

This, I must admit, is a pretty good argument against planting flowers in terrace beds. On the other hand, being a flower lover, I must stubbornly point out that a few flowers do stay in bloom for months on end. These include marigolds, snapdragons, wax begonias, salvia and patience.

Another way to grow flowers on a terrace is to manage the bed like any other flower bed: plant it with an assortment of flowers which bloom in different seasons. Thus you can have a continually changing array of flowers from the time the daffodils bloom in the spring until the chrysanthemums die down in the fall.

Espaliers

An espalier is a plant trained to an artificial but ornamental two-dimensional shape. That is to say, it has height and width but no depth. In gardens, espaliers are sometimes used to create fences. But on terraces they are almost always silhouetted against walls. The effect is beautiful. The plant suggests a strongly textured painting and actually takes up very little more space on the terrace than a painting would.

Some of the trees and shrubs which lend themselves to espaliering are noted in the preceding lists. In addition, vines which grow by twining or by means of holdfasts can be trained as espaliers, though they are not properly called espaliers.

218

Although this terrace
was placed behind the house
to encompass a view of
rolling countryside, two
superbly planted and
maintained perennial
borders with a fountain at
the end give the view tough
competition. The low wall
around the terrace helps to
define it and is also just the
right height for sitting.
Pictures were taken in
late October when the
fountain had been shut off
and much of the furniture
taken in.

Japanese yew makes an excellent espalier. Here it is trained to a trellis which can be taken down when the house needs painting.

The easiest way to espalier plants is to buy them ready-made. But there's no difficulty about doing the job yourself. Set the plant about 6 in. out from a wall and decide the shape you want to create. Then, as the plant makes growth, select young branches or stems which are growing in the desired direction and fasten them to the wall at 8- to 12-in. intervals. Use raffia, thick twine or narrow strips of cloth, and don't tie them so tightly around the branches that you restrict the flow of sap. Cut out all the other branches and rub off unwanted twigs and buds with your thumb.

The basic shaping of an espalier should be done in the early spring while the plant is dormant, but all unwanted growth must be removed as it appears throughout the growing season. When the plant finally attains the desired shape and size, further growth is prevented by removing the growing tips of the branches.

Espaliers need the same treatment as normally growing plants, but you should be very sparing in your applications of fertilizer; otherwise you will stimulate too much growth.

220

How to Plant Plants on and Next to the Terrace

The actual planting technique is no different from that used in planting elsewhere in the garden. But steps must be taken to keep the soil in the planting beds and pockets from drifting onto the terrace. And if your children use the terrace as a play space, steps should also be taken to protect smaller plants from being run over.

The easiest way to keep the soil in place is to lower the level of the planting beds and pockets an inch below the terrace paving. If you make a practice of mulching the plants—a very good idea because it keeps down weeds, holds in moisture and keeps dry soil from blowing across the terrace—the level of the beds and pockets should be lowered an additional 2 or 3 in. to allow for a mulch layer of that thickness.

Planting is often needed to soften lines between the terrace floor and the house walls. This corner is effectively filled with periwinkle edged with dwarf box. Note that even though the duplex outlet under the window is of the weatherproof type, it is placed so low that it will be covered by snow and will in time probably leak.

Another way to keep soil off the terrace is to surround all planting beds and pockets with a low (about 2-in.) curb. However, someone may stumble over this.

To protect plants against traffic, raise the planting beds above the terrace floor. This is done simply by building walls around the planting space and filling in behind them with soil to within 1 in. of the top of the walls. The walls are usually built of masonry but can be made of decay-resistant timbers. They should be from 12 to 30 in. high. Anything lower reduces protection for the plants and is too easy for people to trip over. Anything higher makes cultivation and care of the plants difficult.

18 Container Gardening on the Terrace*

There are various ways to decorate a terrace.

The lady who owns the terrace shown on page 181 did it by painting a mural on one wall. And she added further to the interest and beauty of the area by populating it with a pair of white cockatoos.

Other people use sculpture or mobiles or sundials or handsome rocks or pieces of driftwood.

But the favorite decorating ploy of most terrace owners is to put pretty plants in containers. Thus in one fell swoop they bring to the terrace color, texture, form and sometimes fragrance, and they tighten the link between the terrace and surrounding world.

Other reasons why gardening in containers is so popular are: (1) It's relatively inexpensive. (2) You can change the decorating scheme of the terrace whenever you wish. You're not bound to any given arrangement, as you are when you plant in beds. (3) Even if your terrace is shady, you can get fine bloom from sun-loving plants by shifting them back and forth every few days between the terrace and a sunny spot in the garden. In the same way, you can get good results from shade-loving plants on a sunny terrace.

What Containers to Use

A good container is large enough to give plant roots a chance to grow. Generally, when plants are planted singly, the container should be about as deep as it is wide. Annuals and perennials go into containers that are 6 to 8 in. in diameter. Large perennials and vines need 10- to 12-in. containers. Small shrubs, such as azaleas and lantana, need 12- to 18-in. containers. Medium-size shrubs, such as camellias, rhododendrons, viburnums, boxwood and conifers, need 18- to 24-in. containers or larger.

The container must have the weight and/or proportions that will keep it upright when planted. This means simply that if you are planting tall-growing plants, you should put them either in squat, fairly wide pots or in heavy pots; otherwise, they may easily be

* The major part of this chapter is taken from my earlier book, *Gardening with Ease* (Macmillan, 1970).

blown or knocked over. Similarly, heavy spreading plants need low pots.

The container must be durable if you want to use it for any length of time. And the container must provide bottom drainage so that the soil does not become waterlogged and sour. Such drainage is made possible by holes in the bottom of the container. Small containers that do not have such holes are often used but definitely are not desirable. Very large containers without bottom drainage are also undesirable; however, if they have enough depth to permit you to provide drainage by other means, they are acceptable.

The following are not essential traits to look for in a container but are highly desirable:

It should be easy to clean. Better still, it should not get dirty too rapidly in the first place.

It should not be so heavy that it adds to the difficulty of lifting and moving the potted plant. This is especially true of containers of 12-in. diameter and over. In larger containers, the soil alone is often too heavy to move.

It should not allow the soil to dry out quickly. Wire baskets lined with sphagnum moss are the worst offenders in this respect. Red-clay pots are also porous enough to allow moisture to escape through the sides.

Which containers come closest to meeting these requirements? There are a number of good ones, but none is perfect.

CLAY POTS   The familiar red-clay pot is excellent from the standpoint of cost; but from the standpoint of maintenance, it does not hold a candle to a glazed pot *that provides bottom drainage* (many do not). The latter is slow to soil and easy to clean. It is somewhat more durable than the red-clay pot, and it loses very little moisture through the sides.

An excellent substitute for the glazed pot is a plastic pot. This has the glazed pot's advantages and, in addition, is much lighter in weight. However, it is not attractive.

WOODEN TUBS AND BOXES   For the most part larger than clay pots, they are consequently used mainly for larger plants. They are not easy to clean, but they are lightweight and hold in moisture quite well. They also have enough insulating value to keep the soil from heating up excessively on very hot days.

All wooden containers must be made of decay-resistant wood,

An inviting entrance terrace is planted almost solidly around the edges with pretty shrubs and flowers in containers.

One of the advantages of gardening in containers is that you can cluster your plants or separate them— whatever you think at the moment will make the terrace most attractive.

such as redwood or cypress. They must be secure at the joints. And the bottom should be raised off the ground to prevent rotting.

Unpainted containers are preferable. True, they become discolored. But painted containers almost always require repainting every year or two because the finish is peeled off by the moisture in the wood.

If you build plant boxes or other types of large wooden containers, you should make them of 1-in.-thick redwood or cypress, and fasten the boards together with long brass screws. Provide five ½-in. drainage holes per square foot of bottom area.

BARRELS   These containers are primarily for very large plants, such as small trees. Use only the kind that is made to hold liquid (old whiskey barrels, for example). The hoops are likely to rust out before the wood decays.

CONCRETE TUBS   They are usually very large. Some are more or less shallow and saucer-shaped; others are deep and roomy. They meet none of the requirements outlined above; but for very large plants or for large plantings of small plants, they are almost indispensable.

OTHER CONTAINERS   The list is endless. Some of the containers are excellent; some are bad. If you bear in mind the essential and

226

desirable features of a container, you will not have much trouble in making a wise selection.

HANGING CONTAINERS   The most familiar type is a lightweight basket made of wire or plastic mesh lined with green papier-mâché which is, in turn, lined with sphagnum moss. But you can use anything that holds soil and can be hung by chains or wires.

What Soil to Use

Every pot gardener has his favorite soil mixture (or mixtures). I recommend the oldest and simplest:

2 parts good garden loam
1 part coarse sand
1 part humus (probably peat moss unless you have a supply of something just as good)

This mixture can be used for the majority of plants; but it is easily changed to suit the special requirements of the minority by doubling the volume of sand or the volume of humus. Typical plants requiring a very sandy potting mixture are the cacti and succulents. Those requiring a very humusy mixture are begonias, ferns, bananas, and the like. To make soil acid for rhododendrons, azaleas, camellias, etc., add 1 teaspoonful of powdered sulfur to each container under 12-in. diameter.

The best way to mix soil for potting is to pour all the ingredients, while dry, into a pile on a flat surface and turn them over and over with a shovel. When the mixture is uniform, add water in small quantities and continue turning until the soil is just damp enough to hold together when you squeeze it in your hand. It is now ready for use.

Potting a Plant

If the container has been used, your first step must be to scrub it well with soap and water to remove lurking microbes. Clay pots (new ones as well as old) should then be soaked for several hours in clear water in order to fill the pores.

Cover the drainage holes on the inside of the container with one or two shards (pieces of broken pot). Then pour in a layer of coarse drainage material, such as gravel or pebbles. In containers under 10-in. diameter, a ½-in. layer is sufficient; in larger containers, use 1 in. or more. (In containers that do not have bottom drainage holes, you need about 1 in. of drainage material in containers under 6-in. diameter; 2 in. in those under 12-in. diameter; and 3 in. or more in larger containers.)

227

Fill the container about halfway with potting soil; set in the plant and spread out its roots; and fill in around it with additional soil. Firm the soil, but not so much that water will not penetrate. The crown of the plant should be at the soil level; and for ease in watering, the soil should be ½ to 1 in. below the rim of the container (less in small containers, more in large).

If the potting soil is damp to start with, little additional water is needed for newly potted plants. It is a good idea, however, to pour a little starter solution (dilute liquid fertilizer) around small plants.

Keep seedlings and other bare-root plants out of direct sunlight for a day or two after they are potted: they may not survive otherwise. Large plants that have a ball of earth around the roots do not need this protection.

Repotting
Plants need to be repotted when their roots fill the container. In some cases, the roots start growing out through the bottom drainage holes. In many other cases, the only way to determine the condition of the roots is to set a container on its side, rap the walls with your knuckles or a stick to loosen the rootball, and then slide out the rootball. If the ball is almost completely covered with fine white roots, the plant is probably "pot-bound" and should be repotted.

Still another way to tell when a plant needs repotting is to observe its performance. If it stops making growth in the spring or summer (when it usually should be growing vigorously), the chances are that it wants more root room.

When a plant does need repotting, shift it into a container that is only a little larger than the previous container. If you're using conventional pots, the rule is to move the plant into the next-size-larger pot. If you're using other types of container, the new container should be about 1 in. wider and 1 in. deeper than the old.

The actual process of repotting consists of the following simple operations: Place a layer of drainage material in the bottom of the new container. Slide the rootball out of the old container, and remove some of the drainage material that is stuck on the bottom; but do not loosen the soil around the sides of the ball. Hold the rootball in the center of the new container, and pack fresh soil in around it. Apply a little fertilizer and water well.

Part of the fun of container gardening is in collecting attractive and interesting containers.

If a plant needs repotting but you cannot find a larger container for it, slide out the rootball and carefully pick off about ½ in. of soil from all sides. Use a dull knife or a manicurist's orange stick. Trim off the exposed ends of the roots with a sharp knife or shears. Then replace the rootball in the container and fill it with fresh soil.

Replacing Soil

Sometimes a potted plant stops growing even though its roots still have plenty of room to grow. If nothing else seems wrong, the chances are that the soil has worn out.

Soil fatigue is a common problem for pot gardeners; and in small containers especially it is rather difficult to prevent. But it's nothing to worry about. All you have to do is slide the plant out of its container, pry about half of the soil out of the rootball and then repot in fresh soil.

Fertilizing

Regular application of plant food not only keeps pot plants growing well but also eliminates one of the reasons why potting soil needs to be replaced.

The time to fertilize is when the plants are making growth, not when they are resting (in a dormant or semidormant condition). Make the first application in the early spring and repeat at 2- to 3-month intervals until growth starts to slow down. Light applications are better than heavy. Follow the directions of the fertilizer manufacturer.

Liquid fertilizers are no more nutritious than dry powders; but I prefer them for pot plants because they are easier to apply and the nutrients they contain are instantly available to the plant roots. You are also less likely to apply an overdose.

Watering

There are just two rules to follow: (1) apply water as soon as possible after the soil surface dries out; (2) water each plant until the water starts to trickle out the bottom of the container. Beyond this, it makes no difference what time of day you water. Neither does it do harm to get the foliage wet so long as it has a chance to dry off before nightfall.

The frequency with which pot plants must be watered is a problem, however. Soil in pots dries out much more rapidly than that in a flower bed or shrubbery border. In hot, dry weather, in fact, outdoor pot plants often need to be watered every day and sometimes even twice a day.

230

What can be done about this? Not too much, but here are several points worth considering:

1. Potted plants exposed to wind dry out faster than those in protected spots.

2. Plants in the sun dry out faster than those in the shade.

3. If you group a number of pots close together, each plant helps to shade its neighbor to some extent and this helps to slow evaporation of water.

4. Evaporation from the soil surface can also be retarded by covering the soil with a mulch of peat moss, sawdust, etc.

5. By surrounding the sides and bottom of a container with some sort of insulating material, you can slow the loss of moisture through the container itself. One way to do this is to sink the container in the ground or in a box or planter filled with damp soil, peat moss or sawdust. Another way is to set the container inside a larger container and fill the space between with moss, peat moss, excelsior, etc., which is kept moist.

Protecting Pot Plants Against Wind and Cold

Once you have seen how easily wind can blow over a potted plant—and what a lot of work the accident can cause—you will realize more fully the importance of selecting nontippable containers for your plants. These are much your best protection against wind.

Cold protection is somewhat more difficult to provide. Plants in pots cannot survive very much below-freezing weather even though the same species would be perfectly safe if planted in the garden.

In areas where freezing temperatures are relatively rare, the best way to protect potted plants is simply to move them into a sheltered nook on the terrace or to cover them with burlap or polyethylene film.

In areas where the word "winter" stands for a long period of cold weather, the best way of carrying over perennial plants in pots is to bring them indoors into a sun porch, garage or cold basement. Give evergreens some light, and water all plants only enough to keep the soil from drying out completely.

Another possible solution—but not so reliable—is to sink the containers in the ground outdoors. Mound soil up around deciduous plants. And surround the plants—both deciduous and evergreen—with canvas, polyethylene or tarpaper to break the winds and keep out the worst of the cold.

Protecting Pot Plants Against Insects and Diseases

Pot plants are subject to the same ailments as garden plants, and should be protected in the same way. But this is too big a subject for a nongardening book.

Moving Pot Plants

It's almost inevitable that pot plants will be moved from one location to another—especially if you live in the North, where the plants need indoor protection in winter. This is when large plants become a problem. But here are five ways of solving it:

1. Slip a strong piece of canvas or a large coal shovel under the container and pull it.

2. Mount wooden containers on casters.

3. Mount casters on a piece of thick plywood to make a dolly for rolling containers here and there. Or buy a ready-made dolly of the same type.

4. To move a container across a lawn, roll it on three or four rollers made of short lengths of 2- or 3-in. iron pipe.

5. If you have a number of large plants, buy a small hand truck similar to that used by moving men.

SELECTED ANNUALS FOR POTTING

AGERATUM   Compact plants to about 8 in., they are covered with blue flowers. Sun or light shade.

DAHLIA   Plant dwarf types such as Unwin's hybrids. They grow to 18 in., with flowers in various shapes and many colors. Needs sun.

FORGET-ME-NOT   *Myosotis.* 12 in. Profuse blue or white flowers. Most varieties grow in partial shade but some need sun.

LOBELIA   Tiny blue flowers. Some varieties are compact and grow to 6 in.; others are trailing. Partial shade.

MARIGOLD   *Tagetes.* Use the dwarf types growing to about 1 ft. The yellow pompon flowers are superb. Also in orange and red. Full sun.

PATIENCE   *Impatiens.* These pink, orange, red or white flowers are superb in shade. The commonest varieties grow to 18 in. but there are also dwarfs.

PETUNIA   This is in a class by itself. There are many colors; many sizes up to 15 in. The compact dwarfs and balcony (trailing) types are probably the most useful in containers. Sun.

232

PHLOX   Covered with snowy flowers in red, yellow, pink, or white. 6 to 8 in. Sun.

SCHIZANTHUS   The flowers are like orchids or butterflies—in many colors and marked with contrasting colors. 2 ft. Partial shade.

SWEET ALYSSUM   *Lobularia maritima.* Covered with pink, rose, white or violet flowers. In warm climates bloom lasts almost all year. Up to 8 in. Sun or light shade.

SWEET PEA   *Lathyrus odoratus.* The new dwarfs are only 1 ft. tall and do not require staking. They start blooming earlier and keep on longer than older, larger types. Many colors. Sun.

VERBENA   Red, pink, lavender, white. Grows to 1 ft. and spreads much wider. Needs sun.

SELECTED PERENNIALS FOR POTTING

ARMERIA   A little cushionlike plant to 6 in. Covered with bright pink flowers. Sun.

BIRD OF PARADISE   *Strelitzia.* Huge plant with straplike leaves and exotic orange, blue and white flowers that look like birds. 5 ft. Sun or light shade.

CHINESE LANTERNS   *Physalis.* 2 ft. Grown not for its flowers but for its bright red, lantern-shaped fruits.

CHRYSANTHEMUM   4 ft. but better use smaller varieties. Outstanding perennial with flowers of various sizes and shapes and in almost every color. Blooms in late summer and fall when other plants are petering out. Needs sun.

COLEUS   Grown for its varicolored leaves. Reaches 3 ft. but should be kept lower. Partial shade.

GERANIUM   *Pelargonium.* Geraniums bloom on and on and on; thrive in sun and heat; and are less demanding about moisture than most plants. Showy red, pink, salmon and white flowers. The common geranium grows to 3 ft. Some other types are larger; some are smaller. There are also trailers.

HOSTA   The numerous flower stalks are pleasant, but hosta is grown primarily for its elegant foliage, which may be bright green, greenish-blue or variegated. Use smaller species under 2 ft. Partial shade.

STOKES ASTER   *Stokesia.* 18 in. Large blue or white flowers resembling China asters appear from midsummer on. Sun.

VIOLA   Miniature pansies in many colors blooming throughout the summer. Grows to 1 ft. Sun. (Large pansies are biennials, meaning that they grow from seed one year, bloom the following year and then die. But they also make excellent pot plants when potted up early in the spring.)

Although this California terrace is surrounded by choice shrubs, the owner also decorates it with an assortment of plants in several kinds of containers.

SELECTED BULBS FOR POTTING Most bulbs grow very well in containers. The following are just a few of the best.

ACHIMENES 18 in. Favorites for hanging containers, because they usually trail. Tubular flowers in many colors. Partial shade.

234

AMARYLLIS *Hippeastrum.* Giant flowers resembling lilies in white, red, pink or salmon. 3 ft. Sun.

BEGONIA The tuberous begonias are incredibly beautiful. They are exquisite in both color and shape. 1 ft. Grow in partial shade.

BLOOD LILY *Haemanthus.* 18 in. Very showy small red flowers in large round clusters. Partial shade.

CLIVIA A popular florist's plant with dense foliage and clusters of orange, yellow, red or white flowers. 18 in. Partial shade.

CROCUS Plant a half dozen or so crocus of the same color in a pot, and what a show you have. 6 in. Sun.

CYCLAMEN Another favorite florist's plant. Pretty rounded leaves with beautifully shaped white or pink flowers. Light shade.

DAFFODIL *Narcissus.* As gorgeous in containers as in the garden. Plant lots of them and grow them in full sun.

FREESIA 18 in. These spring-bloomers in many colors are rich in fragrance. Need sun.

GLOXINIA The flowers are large and of the richest blues, purples, reds, pinks and whites you can imagine. 6 in. Partial shade.

HYACINTH *Hyacinthus.* Another very fragrant spring flower forming stiff clusters of showy white, pink, red, blue and purple blossoms. Sun, but can take light shade.

SCILLA Scillas have clusters of tiny, bell-shaped blue or white flowers. Plant range from 4 to 18 in. Partial shade or sun.

TUBEROSE *Polianthes.* 3 ft. Tuberose will fill the terrace with fragrance in late summer. Flowers are waxy and white. Sun.

TULIP *Tulipa.* Try the miniatures and everything else you can lay hands on. Need sun.

SELECTED FERNS FOR POTTING

BIRD'S-NEST FERN *Asplenium nidus.* Undivided fronds are arranged in a clump resembling a bird's nest. 3 ft. Needs partial shade.

CHAIN FERN *Woodwardia.* 6 ft. Soft green fronds. Usually grows in partial shade but tolerates considerable sun.

CLIFF BRAKE *Pellaea.* This leathery fern with dark stalks grows to 2 ft. Partial shade.

HOLLY FERN *Cyrtomium falcatum* Tougher than many ferns and able to withstand more wind, it has glossy leaves shaped

235

something like holly leaves and shaggy stalks. 2 ft. Partial shade.

MAIDENHAIR FERN   *Adiantum.* One of the prettiest ferns, with fronds to 2 ft. The stems are black; the leaflets are more or less fan-shaped and bright green. Partial shade.

POLYSTICHUM   This species produces several evergreen ferns up to 2 ft. tall. Popular names include Christmas fern, mountain holly fern, giant holly fern. Partial shade is needed for all.

SELECTED CACTI AND SUCCULENTS FOR POTTING

These are top-notch container plants because they need somewhat less water and fertilizer than other plants. They look especially attractive in shallow containers. Grow them in a mixture of 1 part loam, 1 part humus and 1 part sand; be sure to put at least 3 in. of coarse drainage material in the bottoms of the containers. Grow in full sun. Apply water in spring and summer, when the plants are growing, and when the soil dries out completely to a depth of ½ in.

AGAVE   This genus includes a number of ornamental, rosette-shaped plants, some very large. The century plant, for instance, has leaves 6 ft. long. Use smaller species.

ALOE   Some of these are huge. Use the dwarfs. Leaves arranged in rosettes. Flowers are red or yellow.

CRASSULA   Another large genus in many sizes. Crassulas have leaves that are fleshy and arranged in a cross shape on the stem. The jade plant is a familiar species. It is shaped like a picturesque tree and has pink flowers.

ECHEVERIA   Hen-and-chickens is a well-known species. Plants grow to 2 ft. in various shapes. All have beautifully colored or textured leaves and some have nice flowers.

EUPHORBIA   A big class of succulents in many shapes. They have thorns, intricate flowers, and a milky sap. Crown-of-thorns, with bright red flowers, is familiar.

HAWORTHIA   Plants grow to 6 in. Some form rosettes; some are column-shaped; some have windows in the leaves.

SEDUM   These hardy succulents come in various shapes. Most are fairly small. Some are trailing. They have yellow flowers.

SEMPERVIVUM   The houseleeks are rosette-shaped and stemless, up to 1 ft. tall. They spread widely. Flowers are white, yellow, pink or purple.

STAPELIA   The flowers are five-pointed and most beautifully colored. Plants grow to 9 in. Some have an unpleasant odor.

SELECTED SHRUBS AND TREES FOR POTTING

Plants that are starred (*) are described in chapter 17. Heights given are for plants growing in the garden. In containers, the same plants are much smaller.

ABELIA, GLOSSY*

ANDROMEDA, JAPANESE*

AZALEA*

BAMBOO   The bamboos are woody grasses that are excellent in large containers because the containers keep them from running wild (as they often do in the garden). There are many kinds to choose from. All are slender, tall and graceful. *Bambusa multiplex* and *Phyllostachys aurea* are two especially recommended for container culture.

BANANA SHRUB   *Michelia fuscata.* This evergreen has small, fragrant, magnolialike flowers that are cream-colored and have a reddish or purplish edging. It grows in partial shade to 15 ft.

CAMELLIA*

CITRUS   Dwarf varieties of oranges, lemons, limes, kumquats and tangelos are superb for pot culture. The trees have glossy, evergreen foliage, fragrant white blossoms and delightful fruits. They grow indoors in winter almost as well as they grow outdoors in summer. Need sun.

DWARF HINOKI CYPRESS   *Chamaecyparis obtusa nana.* 5 ft. Dark-green, mound-shaped evergreen with flat branches in layers.

FATSHEDERA*

FATSIA*

FUCHSIA*

GARDENIA   Ever-so-fragrant evergreen shrub with glossy foliage and a profusion of waxy white flowers. 6 ft. Needs sun.

HEAVENLY BAMBOO*

HIBISCUS, CHINESE*

HOLLY*

JUNIPER   *Juniperus* species. Use varieties that stay under 2 ft: *J. conferta, J. horizontalis, J. procumbens aurea, J. procumbens nana, J. squamata,* for example. Needled evergreens. All need sun.

LANTANA   Evergreen or deciduous. Up to 4 ft. They produce clusters of flowers in various colors. Sun.

237

LOQUAT   *Eriobotrya japonica.* Evergreen tree with handsome leathery leaves, fragrant white flowers and edible yellow fruits. 20 ft. Sun.

MAGNOLIA, SOUTHERN*

MAPLE, JAPANESE*

NATAL PLUM*

NORFOLK ISLAND PINE   *Araucaria excelsa.* A slim symmetrical needled evergreen tree with neatly tiered branches. In nature it grows huge, but you can hold it to 10 ft. in a container. Partial shade.

OLEANDER*

OLIVE   *Olea europaea.* Attractive broadleaf evergreen with gray-green, willowy leaves and blackish fruits. Grows to 25 ft. and often has a picturesquely gnarled trunk. Needs sun.

PALM   Among the best palms for use in large containers are the sentry palms, pigmy date palm and lady palm.

PEACH*   Dwarf varieties grow only 4 ft. tall but bear a sizable crop of full-size fruits.

PINE, MUGO*

PINEAPPLE GUAVA   *Feijoa sellowiana.* A spreading broadleaf evergreen shrub, to 12 ft., it has showy purple-and-red flowers and edible gray-green fruits. Foliage is gray-green on top, silvery underneath. Needs sun.

PITTOSPORUM, JAPANESE*

PODOCARPUS   A very graceful conifer with pendulous branches and dense, willowlike leaves. 20 ft. Sun or partial shade.

POMEGRANATE   For pot culture, use *Punica granatum nana.* This is a deciduous shrub only 3 ft. tall and bushy. Has small inedible orange fruits. Sun.

RHODODENDRON*

ROSE*

ROSEMARY   *Rosemarinus officinalis.* Evergreen shrub to 6 ft. Narrow, aromatic, two-colored leaves and clusters of small blue flowers. Sun.

SKIMMIA, REEVES*

SPRUCE   The dwarf forms suitable for containers include *Picea abies gregoryana, P. abies maxwellii, P. abies nidiformis, P. glauca conica* and *P. excelsa pygmaea.* All need sun.

SWEET BAY   *Laurus nobilis.* Compact, cone-shaped evergreen tree growing to 8 ft. in containers but more in the garden. Sun.

**SELECTED VINES
FOR POTTING**

Those starred are described in chapter 17.

ASPARAGUS   This is often called asparagus fern but really is two forms of vine. Both have delicate, airy foliage on stems as much as 20 ft. long. Train them upward or allow them to trail. Partial shade.

CLEMATIS*

CUP-AND-SAUCER VINE   *Cobaea scandens.* Though this can be grown as a perennial in warm climates, it is best treated as an annual. It has bell-shaped violet flowers and grows to 25 ft. Sun.

IVY, ENGLISH*

MOONFLOWER   *Calonyction aculeatum.* Perennial best treated as an annual. Related to the morning glory, it has white or purple flowers that bloom at night and stay open until the following noon. Sun.

MORNING GLORY*

QUAMOCLIT   Also called cypress vine, this is an annual with red-and-white flowers and fernlike foliage. 10 ft. Sun.

WAX PLANT   *Hoya carnosa.* Evergreen with elegant foliage and fragrant, waxy white or pinkish flowers. 10 ft. Sun.

Index